BICYCLE BREAKS
Between London and the Sea

Martin Ryle

Impact Books

First published in Great Britain 1991
by Impact Books, 112 Bolingbroke Grove, London SW11 1DA

ISBN 0 245–60332–8

Acknowledgements
Cover photograph
Courtesy of East Anglia Tourist Board Collection

Typeset by Photoprint, Torquay, Devon.
Printed by The Guernsey Press Co. Ltd., Guernsey, Channel Islands.

Contents

Preface

This book gives details of a dozen routes for cyclists within south-east England and East Anglia. Many of the routes are circular tours. Some are day trips, and others last two or three days. All begin and end at railway stations on lines currently offering convenient, free travel for accompanied bicycles.

The routes will appeal to experienced cycle-tourists as well as to new cyclists who are looking for guidance in getting the most from their machines, and seeking scenic, quiet country riding. Use of A roads is kept to an absolute minimum, and B roads too are avoided as far as possible. This really is riding on leafy, car-free lanes.

For newcomers to cycling, there is practical advice on choosing, riding and maintaining your bike, whether an ATB or a conventional touring machine.

The detailed narratives which accompany the routes will help readers find rides which meet their personal needs and preferences. Armchair travellers may enjoy them too. They give a sense of the pleasures of cycle-touring, and show that there is still some little-known country to be explored even in this crowded south-eastern corner of England.

I would like to thank Jean-Luc Barbanneau at Impact Books for encouraging me in this project from the start, and Peter Cartwright for preparing the maps. For hospitality en route, thanks to Cym and Susy Ryle, and to the family from Birmingham who gave me hot tea at six in the morning when my tent blew down at Wells, Norfolk.

Bill and Maggie Rayment, now of Lewes Cycles, have continued to run the ideal bike shop: thanks to them for friendly and dependable service.

My expeditions were made more pleasurable by the company, at different times, of Kate Soper, of our son Jude, and of Geoff Aldred. Thanks to Geoff, too, for helping me begin to understand something about buildings and the stone they are made of.

This book is dedicated to my parents, with love and in grateful memory of childhood holidays at Barkhale and in France.

Martin Ryle, September 1990

1. The Way I Rode

If you had been standing at the A148/A149 roundabout outside King's Lynn on 7 September 1989, just as the evening rush got under way, you might have noticed a rather heavily laden bicycle – a Falcon, blue, 25-inch frame, showing its age but still serviceable – make its way through the junction and down to the Grimston turn-off. Front panniers, rear panniers, sleeping bag, tent, five-litre water carrier: some serious expedition. The rider looked worried. What was on his mind?

I was the rider, and I was asking myself if this whole project, of looking for quiet rides within a couple of hours' train journey from London, was not perhaps a mistake. This traffic was awful. Perhaps nowhere in Britain, except the rough upland tracks, could still offer extensive 'quiet rides'. Perhaps my own recollection of rural seclusion in Kent and Sussex, all those lanes within a few hours of home where I had so often cycled, was a delusion, and even my vivid images of Brightling and Mayfield, just last spring, were false. Had the golden sun and the leaves 'delicate-filmed as new-spun silk' (as Hardy observes) dazzled and bewildered me to such an extent that a few moments of calm, respites from traffic, had been transformed in my memory into long stretches of quiet country?

In which case this enterprise would have to be abandoned. I had already seen enough guides and

itineraries which lured unsuspecting cyclists onto the
dangerous and horrible highways of the south-east, and I
was not going to add to their number. Quiet lanes or
nothing, and if there were no quiet lanes left, between
London and the sea, I would look further afield.

Birches and oak, autumnal bracken, a blaze of heather.
Breckland, away to the east, must look like this (where
there are no forests). However: don't expect heath as you
turn north (now) and head towards the sea. Arable – corn,
beet – with strips and patches of copse. Will it be dullish?
If the traffic thins out (it's thinning out), will the
landscapes disappoint me? This must be Peddar's Way, a
long-distance path, rough, sandy, deserted. Unrideable
(loose, shifting, tussocky). Quiet now on the surfaced road,
even though it is a B road. A few steps up Peddar's Way,
scaring a rabbit, a few steps down, seeing how the line of
the Way marks out field boundaries for miles, and then
back on the bike. Back into that easy work, that effortless
effort, of pedalling, which (except when you have to climb)
comes so much easier than running, easier almost than
walking.

Into the lanes. Dropping past Fring. Hardly a car now.
This is it. This is that other country which does not lie
'further afield', beyond some frontier, but here and now: in
among the A roads, their bright red grid on the maps, you
dive, swing, into that other space. Then you surface. This
is it: the wide grass verges beyond Fring, the still
unploughed stubble, the copses between lane and
ploughland, the pheasants which run, squawking, across
the brown and yellow stalks as I lower my bike in the field
entrance and undo my panniers and set about making the
first cup of tea of this Norfolk trip.

Eleven months later, 750 miles on, at Pallingham Quay

Farm on the Arun in West Sussex, between Billingshurst and Pulborough, the last of these rides – the most south-westerly, as the first Norfolk rides had been the most north-easterly – approached its close. And with it, the making of this book. If you had been at Pallingham Quay Farm . . . not that anyone is ever there: the buildings have the intensely quiet, faintly mournful water-meadows to themselves.

My son Jude, accompanying me for the second time in these dozen expeditions, was with me. Looking back, I knew that I had enjoyed myself most, much as I like solitude, when I had had a companion – Jude, Kate, Geoff. (The one exception had been that marvellous ride up across blue-skied Kent, from the Weald through the clay vale onto the Downs and back, which I had made alone at the start of May.)

New memories. Norfolk and East Sussex, in September and October last autumn. A glowingly bright, warm February day, back in the spring, when I had sat in shirt sleeves on the parapet of a bridge, in meadows not unlike these, below Burwash, making coffee, stretching in the sun. Icy April night ('coldest night for three years' a Marsh farmer had told us, plausibly, the next day) when Geoff and I had sat, shivering, warming our wine in the ashes of our huge beech campfire, in the secret folded escarpment of the North Downs just east of Wye and the Kentish Great Stour. And many other memories, from Sussex and Kent and Suffolk, from May and June and August.

So it was true, and I had proved it, that this other world does still exist: in the interstices, in the gaps between the transmission lines of modernity. With a little care, you can spend days there on your bicycle – less than a hundred miles (less, sometimes, than fifty miles) from London.

2. Practicalities: Becoming a Cycle-Tourist

The rides described in this book offer a varied sample of the pleasures of cycling and cycle-touring. There is plenty here for experienced cyclists, as well as newcomers: the countryside within a hundred miles of London has surprises, and new pleasures, even for those who know it.

Chapter 3 explains how to choose your route, and gives some advice about planning your trip. If you are new to cycling, you will also need some preliminary guidance (which other readers can skip) on choosing, setting up, riding and maintaining your machine. These are topics on which it is possible to write at length. You may or may not find the mechanics of cycling and bike maintenance interesting in its own right. If you do, and if you intend to become proficient in do-it-yourself bike repair, you will need to consult one of the many manuals available (a couple are mentioned in the Booklist). However, the essentials can be summed up quite briefly. You can enjoy cycling and, providing you go to a good bike shop, you can confidently choose a bicycle, without any great technical expertise.

Choosing Your Bicycle

The first step in buying a bicycle is to find a good shop specialising in quality lightweight machines. Avoid

chainstores and discount warehouses, which do not offer
the friendliness and expertise of independent dealers and
which generally provide inadequate service and repair
facilities. The owners of your local specialist shop will not
be delighted when, having bought your bike at a cut-price
store, you bring it round to them as soon as problems
develop. Ask cycling friends and acquaintances to
recommend a shop, and go there even if it means
travelling a few miles from home.

Once you have found a reliable shop, the essential
choice you must make is whether to buy a conventional
touring bicycle or an ATB (all-terrain bike, or mountain
bike). For the routes given in this book, and for riding on
lanes generally, a touring bike fits the bill. There are
stretches of unsurfaced trackway in most of the routes, but
none of these lasts very long, and in every case but one an
alternative route on lanes is given or is obvious on the OS
maps. So a mountain bike is certainly not essential.

Some people will opt for an ATB anyway – because they
plan to ride off-road quite a bit, or because they like the
style/image. A good quality mountain bike is adaptable
and will give pleasant enough riding on surfaced roads.
However, at the risk of annoying ATB fans, let me put in
a word for the conventional lightweight tourer. A quality
touring bike is a brilliantly engineered purpose-built
machine. While it is obviously less suitable than an ATB
for ploughing through mud or bumping over baked clay, it
is just as obviously *more* suitable for on-the-road riding.
Anyone used to touring on narrow high-pressure tyres,
which can give you a firm, positive, airy, bird-like sense of
speed and lightness, will find a mountain bike's wide
knobbly tyres rather horrible: personally I would liken the
ride they give to wading through treacle.

Whether you choose a mountain bike or a tourer, you

will find high quality, mass-produced models available from a range of manufacturers, all of whom produce reliable, attractive machines in what is a very competitive market. For between £250 and £300 (1990 prices), you will get a touring bicycle with a genuinely lightweight frame, ten- or twelve-speed gears, and light, reliable components. An equally good ATB will cost a little more. Either machine, properly maintained, will give you many thousands of trouble-free miles. The frame will last indefinitely and moving parts will need only infrequent, and relatively inexpensive, replacement. Few mass-produced items offer such good value as quality bikes.

You will see 'sports bikes' and other machines offered at well below the prices mentioned above. You could also buy a reasonably built 'light tourer' or commuting bicycle (probably, among other things, with five rather than ten or twelve gears) for less. But you only get what you pay for – it is impossible to build a good bike at rock-bottom prices. Buying the cheapest 'tourer' you can see – anything that looks OK and has ten gears – is a recipe for discontent, frustration and trouble, and the same applies with ATBs. It is wise to wait awhile and save the money for a good machine rather than rushing to buy something cheaper. Alternatively, consider buying a well-maintained second-hand bike, which can offer better value, and durability, than a new, cheap one. But take a knowledgeable friend along to look over that second-hand 'bargain'. . . .

Modern mass-produced bicycles from the best makers are so good that it is hardly worthwhile investing in a hand-built machine – though to own one must be a great pleasure. What *is* worthwhile is checking that the bicycle you opt for meets the tourist's need for good low gears: some of the touring bikes on sale are geared surprisingly high (this will not apply with ATBs). Consult with the dealer, who should be prepared to fit a new freewheel block and (if necessary) gear mechanism to provide you with those low ratios. My own new bike, a Peugeot Camargue, came fitted with a smaller front chainring with thirty-eight teeth, and the largest rear sprocket has thirty-four teeth, which gives a really low and useful first gear. Its predecessor, however, a Falcon (which served me well for years and which I still use for running in and out of town), needed a new freewheel fitted before it gave me the low gears I wanted. If the dealer does change the gear set-up, it will add a little to the bike's list price, but the small investment will pay off on long hills or when you have a heavy load.

Another refinement which will add extra quality and durability to a new touring bicycle is a hand-built rear wheel. This is a particularly valuable 'extra' if you are large and/or expect to carry large loads. Spoke breakages are a nuisance, and a wheel built by a skilled maker will minimise or eliminate them. Ideally, your custom-made back wheel should have forty spokes, but EC 'harmonisation' makes 40-spoke rims and hubs hard to find. For no good reason, identical 36-spoke front and rear rims and hubs are now the norm, even though every cyclist knows that the back wheel carries most of the weight and does most of the work.

Whether or not you modify the machine you buy, let me repeat that the first step is to go to a reliable shop. Here you will get advice not just on the best machine for your money but on the right frame size for your body. You will be able to go back for after-sales service and to have any problems sorted out; and, later on, for routine maintenance and the fitting of replacement parts.

If you already own a bicycle, perhaps a sturdy old commuter/shopper or a cheap but rideable machine which you would like to get more out of, you may wonder whether it will do for a weekend's touring. Obviously even the most basic bike, if it will get you to the shops and back, will get you further. It would certainly be worth setting off into the lanes and seeing if you, and the machine, enjoy the ride. A reasonable quality 'commuter' bike should give pleasant enough riding over flat country, but once you encounter hills or carry much of a load, then a wider range of gear ratios, a true lightweight frame, and quality lightweight components all become very desirable. By all means begin cycling on any roadworthy bike you may have, but bear in mind that a better machine will add to your pleasure.

Accessories

A new touring bicycle will come equipped with mudguards and a rear luggage-rack, and may also carry brazed-on fittings for a bottle and bottle-cage. Mudguards are useful for wet-weather riding, though off the road they can be a pest, collecting mud and jamming the wheels – which is why mountain bikes generally don't have them. A luggage-rack is not so much useful as essential, at any rate if you plan to take trips lasting more than a day. For day trips, a saddle- or handlebar-bag suffices. Safety and comfort alike should discourage you from carrying a rucksack, even if it claims to be designed for cycling. A luggage-rack (not fitted as standard on most ATBs, though specially designed mountain bike racks can be bought) makes it easy to carry all you need for a weekend break, either in panniers – expensive, but luxurious – or in strong bags securely fastened to the carrier.

Short breaks require only a minimum of equipment:

spare clothing and waterproofs, basic toolkit, a picnic. If you want to carry rather more, perhaps taking along a primus or portable gas stove and some cooking pots to heat soup or make tea, then panniers come into their own. There is a range of styles and sizes and prices. As with bikes themselves, the better quality gear does not come cheap – and as with bikes, there is some beautifully practical and hardwearing equipment to be had if you pay for it. Apart from their usefulness when touring, a pair of panniers will hold lots of shopping – and regular trips to the shops are one way of getting and staying reasonably fit and 'bicycle friendly'.

If you decide to give cycle-camping a try, which means taking a tent and a sleeping bag and extra water-carrying vessels, a front carrier and perhaps front panniers too will be worth buying. This will not only increase your storage space, it will also allow you to balance your load better. Most of the weight should go behind you, but if you have a lot of gear it is advisable to put some of it above the front wheel as well.

Bottles carried in cages on the seat tube and/or the down tube are a conveniently accessible and unobtrusive way of carrying water. The larger, one-litre size is worth buying: it is sensible, and reassuring, to have a good supply of drinking water handy as you ride. Clip-on cages can be bought if you have no brazed-on fittings.

All these accessories will be available in a specialist shop. If you get hooked on cycle-touring, you will certainly build up a collection of gear and come to appreciate its uses and its often clever design. However, it is worth emphasising that, to start with, you really need no more than the bike itself, a rear carrier, a stout canvas bag and a couple of elastic straps. That, plus a simple toolkit and a pump (and of course lights if you contemplate riding after dark), will be enough to equip you for your first cycling expedition.

Clothing

From the soles of your feet to the crown of your head, you can if you wish dress in specially styled bike gear. Cyclists, once famous for the drabness of their black alpaca outfits, now revel in dayglo Lycra flamboyance . . . or at least some cyclists do.

Personally I have bought rather few items of special cycle clothing. After ten thousand miles or so of touring, plus innumerable journeys in and out of town (four miles each way), I can speak with confidence when I say that the right choice of ordinary (and ordinarily priced) clothes will for the most part keep you quite comfortable. I should, however, emphasise the *right* choice: just sticking on a pair of jeans and some gymshoes and a baggy sweater will leave you quite uncomfortable.

You need a pair of reasonably stiff shoes on your feet. Trainers will do, but I have recently discovered that I find a pair of lightish leather walking shoes more comfortable (and waterproof) both on and off the bike. The essential thing is to have sufficient thickness and rigidity in the sole to stop the metal of the pedals digging into your feet. Purists will advocate buying special cycling shoes, but these have two drawback: they are costly, and most of them are uncomfortable to walk in, so that if you do wear them you must take another pair of shoes along for off-the-bike use.

Purists will speak up for cycling shorts too, pointing out that their padded seats and close-cut but good-length legs maximise comfort and minimise friction. That may well be so. I have always been happy enough riding in a pair of not-too-short nylon football shorts. I wear tracksuit bottoms on top: unless you are riding in hot sun and/or at full tilt, shorts may strike you as chilly most English mornings. Tracksuit trousers have the great advantage that you can easily slip them off and back on over shorts. They are also more comfortable, hold less water and dry out faster than jeans or cords. I regard them as indispensable.

Between your waist and your neck, you will need several thin layers, topped off perhaps with a windproof jacket in cool weather. Layers can be peeled off as the sun gets up and put back on if it disappears behind clouds or you get cool in long downhill runs. Gloves, essential in winter, can be useful even in summer if you make early starts: your hands are more or less immobile and can easily get cold if you ride through chilly morning air.

Raingear for cyclists means either a cape or a properly waterproof jacket (or jacket plus trousers, but I find waterproof trousers cumbersome and irksome). I positively like capes, which will keep you dry as far down as your knees at least and have a comforting tent-like feel. Drawn up over the brake-levers, spread back over the rear carrier, a nice long cape insulates you from the most insinuating or the most boisterous rain, and will keep your hands warm and much of your load dry too. Capes do catch the wind, however, and they can affect your dexterity and thus your reaction time: take extra care wearing a cape in traffic. Waterproof jackets are more streamlined, but they will make you sweat and feel damp unless you pay a fair bit for Gore-Tex or something similar. They won't protect your legs or hands or give you that tent-like glow.

One way or another, make sure you have properly rainproof gear. Being wet on a bicycle is unnecessary, and it is dangerous as well as uncomfortable, for once you are wet you easily get cold and once you are cold you lose alertness and concentration. You may well hope to stick to fair-weather cycling, which is a plausible hope in the south-east: the weather is generally dry in summer, slow to change, and accurately forecast for forty-eight hours. For all that, it is as well to Be Prepared.

On my head, I wear a safety helmet. It is not beautiful, but it is reasonably light and cool. Despite the ventilation holes, a safety helmet is fairly waterproof and usefully deflects drips and drops of rain away from your neck, where they soon work their way down into your clothes. More importantly, all the statistics show that a safety helmet much reduces your chance of serious injury should you be so unfortunate as to meet with an accident.

Fitness and Safety

Some of the rides in this book involve climbs likely to get even experienced cyclists off their bikes and pushing, while others – the East Anglian rides – are very largely on the flat. Even these flatter rides will be no fun if you are unfit and unused to riding a bicycle. While some of the routes, and some stretches of others, make ideal introductions to cycle-touring (see Chapter 3), you would be very well advised to do some gentle 'running in' before you attempt even the most modest expedition.

This need not mean weight-training and riding twenty miles each evening after you have finished work and/or given the kids their tea. Because cycling is such an efficient mode of transport, much less tiring than running, you need only be reasonably fit to find it pleasant. There is absolutely no need to slog up the steepest hills or aim for seventy miles a day: get off and push when you want to, keep distances down to whatever you find enjoyable.

To get reasonably fit, while acquiring the skills (and muscles) needed for cycling, your best strategy, obviously, is to cycle regularly. If there is a shortish journey (say three to six miles each way) that you make frequently over fairly quiet roads – to work, to the shops, to the station – then you can cycle it instead of using public transport or driving. Otherwise you will need to find some reasonably pleasant circular run through quiet lanes or backstreets which you can use as a 'training ride' (I put the phrase in inverted commas to distinguish this kind of thing from the breakneck thirty-mile stints up and down A roads which racing cyclists go in for). No one likes riding in the wet, and riding in the dark is to be avoided if possible, so winter can be a more restrictive time, but from March to September you should find it possible to put in twenty or thirty miles a week without too much disruption. That sort of mileage, so long as you keep it up regularly, will within a few weeks make you fit enough to enjoy a day or more touring.

You may need to lose some weight and improve your general physical condition before you can enjoy even a short ride. It would be hypocritical of me to say you must stop smoking – but of course you ought to. Cycling will certainly help you to feel good: skin, muscle tone, breathing, posture, pulse-rate: what will the bicycle not improve?

Regular cycling is also essential if you are to gain confidence in handling your machine on the road and in traffic. The routes in this book avoid all but short stretches of main roads, but you cannot expect continuous car-free riding even in the lanes. Regular practice in cautious but positive riding, keeping well out from the kerb, claiming your road space, and anticipating the actions (including the follies) of other road users, will prepare you to enjoy your leisure cycling and feel happy doing it.

Some special safety precautions apply when you set off on a tour. If you are in a party, remember to keep well apart, especially on downhill runs. If you are carrying luggage, see that it is well strapped down so that nothing – including the straps! – can get caught in spokes or wheels. Make sure that you leave with your bike in good mechanical order (see the next section). However good the weather and the forecast, take some warm and waterproof clothes if you are going for more than a day trip: rain might come.

Try to stop regularly for meals. 'Little and often', the books say, is the motto for cyclists' eating, and while I'm not sure about the 'little' I can vouch for the wisdom of the 'often'. The routes in this book take you past plenty of shops and pubs, but it is still a good idea to have some easily-eaten snack with you, in case you get suddenly hungry. Keep your water bottle(s) filled: petrol stations and, often, churchyards have accessible taps.

Avoid sunburn in hot weather. Wear bright clothes and use panniers with reflective strips: good advice not only on a tour but at all times.

Maintenance and Repairs

A good ATB or lightweight touring bicycle is a very reliable machine and there is no need to anticipate tedious and complex breakdowns. In fact, those aspects of cycle repair and maintenance which *are* tedious and complex – stripping down headsets and bottom brackets to replace or regrease parts or bearings, for instance – can well be left to a professional, unless you actually enjoy them. This kind of major maintenance, and the replacement of worn parts (chains and chainsets and pedals, freewheels, gear and brake sets), need not and will not interfere with a cycling holiday or short break, providing you leave with the machine in good condition.

This is the key to trouble-free riding. Whether you do it yourself (with the help of a manual or a knowledgeable friend) or take it to a shop, you should give your bike a thorough examination when the longer days begin, or before, and replace any worn parts. The bike shop will probably be quite pleased to do this for you in February or March: they may be less pleased in July, when lots of other people will be bringing all manner of bikes in for the same treatment. You cannot expect to get maintenance and repairs done at the drop of a hat in high summer and you must plan ahead rather than leaving things to the last minute.

These jobs of maintenance, replacement and repair are complicated, but infrequent. Chains and freewheels may possibly need replacing annually if you ride a lot in bad weather, but other parts will last for several years.

There are a number of simpler points that you can and should check and attend to yourself. Keep your cycle well lubricated, but not oily. Know how to remove tyre covers and mend or replace inner tubes (most cyclists carry spare tubes so they do not have to rely on puncture repairs carried out at the roadside). New tyre covers will cut down on punctures: I always fit them at the start of a long tour and even for a weekend away it is worth making sure that the back tyre at least is fairly new. Neither tyre should be ancient.

You need to learn how to adjust both front and rear gear changers, using the special adjusting screws, so that the chain runs freely without being thrown clear of either chainwheel or freewheel block. Chains have a habit of lodging themselves with great ease in crannies from which they can be winkled out only with great difficulty, and the only way to control this habit is to keep the chain where it is meant to be: on rather than off the rings and sprockets.

Keep your brakes adjusted so that there is the minimum of slack in the cables. Know how to change both brake and gear cables (and when buying spare cables make sure to get the right type and get the 'wrong end' of the cable cut off if necessary). Always check all cables carefully before setting off, and if any of them shows any sign of wear or fraying, replace it. The same goes for brake blocks: check them, and if they are worn down, replace them. On a longer tour I would recommend carrying spare cables and blocks, but if you have checked them carefully and replaced them if necessary, then this is not so essential on a two- or three-day trip.

You should really also learn how to accomplish one rather more fiddly task: removing and replacing a broken spoke and trueing up the wheel. Even with a hand-built wheel you may just get a spoke breakage. It is pretty unlikely, especially if you are carrying a light load, but it may happen and unfortunately spokes don't show signs of wear in advance (though you can and should run them over before leaving to make sure they are all under even tension and holding the wheel really true). To fix a broken spoke you need a special spoke key or spanner (buy a good one – the cheapest sort don't work and only damage the spoke nipples they are meant to undo). You also need a tool that fits into the freewheel block so that this can be removed using a vice: if you do break a spoke on the freewheel side, you will have to find a farm or garage and ask to borrow their vice. A friend or a repair manual will show you how to do this irksome job, which is however quite satisfying to complete successfully. You probably won't need to call on your skills, but it's as well to have them.

Other tools to be carried even on a short break include spanners, screwdrivers and allen keys to fit all nuts, screws and bolts; a puncture repair kit, plus tyre levers, plus spare tubes; and a length of galvanised wire for emergencies (for instance, if the bolt holding the mudguard stay and carrier falls out because you forgot to check all your bolts for tightness before leaving, you can lash the stays into the hole with a long twist of wire until you reach a bolt shop).

None of this, not even the puncture kit, is likely to be needed during the average short break. But you should be ready to deal with minor problems in case they happen: even in Kent or Sussex, you can find yourself some miles from the nearest bike shop.

3. Practicalities: Planning Your Tour

Whichever route you ride, whichever area you visit, some advance planning will make a cycle-tour more enjoyable. Apart from choosing your route and tracing it out on the OS map(s) (dealt with later in this chapter), you need to get yourself and your bicycle to the start, and you have to decide on and organise accommodation. These may seem somewhat routine considerations, but a little guidance will be helpful, especially if you are new to cycle-touring or unfamiliar with the south-east and its railways.

Bikes by Train

All the routes in this book begin and end at railway stations and in each case a note is included of the London terminus from which the station can be reached. Travelling by train to the start of your ride gets your holiday off to a relaxed beginning. Once you have made your way to the terminus (leave plenty of time and walk rather than ride if you are not used to busy London streets), it is pleasant to sit back, look at your maps, and take it easy for a while. None of the stations used is more than two and a half hours from London, most are less than two, and some are under one hour. All of them are well clear of suburbia and some of them – Wickham Market in Route 4, Frant in Route 6, Crowhurst in Route

9 – are within minutes of peaceful countryside.

If you are travelling from outside London, it may or may not be possible to take trains that avoid the capital. Sussex and Kent can be reached from the west and south-west via Southampton and Brighton and via Reading and Gatwick, for instance, while East Anglia can be reached from the Midlands and the North via Peterborough and Ely. Check at your local station for the most practical and restful itinerary.

You may decide that you would rather transport your bike(s) by car. Many of the routes given either are, or can easily be made into, circular tours, so you can return to your starting point on the bike itself. Alternatively, car drivers can use the train just for the journey from the end back to the beginning of the route – this is usually relatively short and simple.

Bike plus train is a very flexible (and ecologically benign) combination. It is a pity that British Rail makes so little effort to make life easy for cyclists. Inconsistency and complexity put off many would-be customers. On some trains you must book, and on others you cannot (indeed in the summer of 1990 I was told that it was impossible to reserve space for bikes on the Fishguard boat train, an increasingly popular service where space is limited but where, incredibly, a 'first-come first-served' free-for-all operates at Paddington). On some trains you must pay, on others you can go free some of the time, and others are always free. More worrying, for it seems to portend a gradual exclusion of cyclists from trains, some of the new rolling-stock being introduced has very little baggage space, which limits both the number of bikes that can fit on and the times they can be taken: for instance, the Thameslink services between London and Brighton take bicycles only at certain times.

Fortunately, however, in the regions which concern us – Sussex, Kent and East Anglia – cyclists will find the rail network generally straightforward and convenient. South of London there is good coverage of the terrain and on most of the routes frequencies in the daytime mean that missing a train doesn't involve more than an hour's wait for the next one. At the time of writing, none of the rail routes used in this book requires either advance booking or the payment of a fare for your bike. On almost all of them there is ample stowage space in good old-fashioned guards' vans, so there is almost certain to be room for bikes. (The only train I used where space was limited was the Anglia Electrics service to Cambridge from King's Cross, for King's Lynn: on this, my bike had to go in the passenger accommodation. An alternative service to Cambridge and Ely, for King's Lynn, departs from Liverpool Street.)

Wherever possible, I chose stations in Network SouthEast, which offer cheaper off-peak travel for card-holders. By continental standards rail travel in Britain is not cheap but an Awaybreak or day return, especially with a discount, represents reasonable value for money. All the Kent and Sussex rides are either circular or not far off circular, and in the latter cases the return station is a few stops up the line from the starting point, so that a return ticket to the station you start from will be valid from the station you finish at. Check when booking whether it will be cheaper to buy a return ticket or two singles: in the case of day trips, a day return ticket is obviously best.

The East Anglian routes are not circular tours in themselves, but become so if you join up Routes 1 and 2 or Routes 3 and 4, in which case you finish up at your starting point (King's Lynn and Sudbury respectively: both stations are currently in Network SouthEast).

All in all, you should not experience problems taking

your bike on the train for any of these rides. I certainly experienced none. However, there are one or two wise precautions. First of all, once you have decided on a particular route, it is worth contacting your local BR travel centre, or the relevant London terminus, just to check that there are no restrictions or conditions: things may change after this book goes to press. Check, too, that weekend engineering works will not affect your journey should you be travelling at the weekend: substitute bus services will not take bikes. Have a label attached to your machine, giving your itinerary and your name and address: most BR guards have no desire to see such a label, but some of them will insist on one. Finally, it makes sense to get to your departure station early, so that if there are any problems you have time to sort them out, and if space is limited you can put in a priority claim for it.

Accommodation

Excluding luxurious and expensive hotels and inns, accommodation for cycle-tourists falls into three categories: bed and breakfast places (including some cheaper inns and pubs), whose prices start at around £12 per head per night; youth hostels; and camping.

Youth hostels

Youth hostels are cheap and simple, and an attractively gregarious option if you enjoy doing your own cooking and do not mind being deprived of your companions' company at Lights Out. However, they have become rather few and far between outside the major outdoor recreation areas. If you are planning a cycling tour using hostel

accommodation in the south-east, you will find your
options somewhat limited, and will have to construct your
route on the basis of the hostels' locations.

A few hostels do lie near the routes described in this
book, namely King's Lynn and Hunstanton (Routes 1 and
2); Alpheton and Blaxhall (Routes 3 and 4); Telscombe
(Routes 8 and 10); Blackboys (Route 10); and Arundel
(Routes 11 and 12). But these are nearly all near rather
than actually on the routes and, moreover, do not fall
towards the middle of the rides where overnight
accommodation is needed. If you wanted to modify or
extend the tour or stay an extra night at the start or finish,
some of them would be useful, but you would have to
supplement hostels with nights en route spent camping or
bed-and-breakfasting.

Bed and breakfast

Bed and breakfast accommodation is much favoured by
cyclists. It offers good value for money. You get a hot
shower or bath, a comfortable bed, and somewhere safe for
the bike to spend the night too. Next morning you can
make a fairly early start with a good meal inside you (and
no washing up to do).

B and Bs are very plentiful. If you opt to use them, you
will have no problems getting accommodation on any of
the routes given here.

Details of B and Bs, including phone numbers for
booking, can be obtained from several sources. The
English Tourist Board supervises a scheme of registered
and classified B and Bs, and the various regional tourist
boards produce a range of publications including
accommodation lists. These regional boards – addresses for
East Anglia and the South-East are given in the Appendix

– are a useful first contact. The free literature they send to enquirers (which may include tips for cyclists and even some suggested routes) contains the addresses and phone numbers of local Tourist Information Centres (TICs). The TICs can let you have further accommodation lists, and in some cases will book a bed for you. Particularly useful TICs for the routes given here include those at King's Lynn and Wells next the Sea (Routes 1 and 2); Aldeburgh and Sudbury (Routes 3 and 4); Rye and Ashford, Kent (Route 5); Tunbridge Wells (Route 6); Canterbury and Tenterden (Route 7); Lewes (Routes 8 and 10); Hailsham (Route 10); and Arundel and Chichester (Routes 11 and 12).

As well as information from tourist boards and TICs, you can draw on various commercially published bed and breakfast guides. The Cyclists' Touring Club (address in the Appendix) is launching a new guide for 1991, available to the general public as well as to CTC members.

Armed with lists of accommodation for the relevant district, you should consult carefully the route you plan to follow and draw up a shortlist of towns and villages falling at about the point or points where you will be breaking your journey for the night. In determining this, you will obviously need to take account of the hour at which you are likely to begin cycling on the first day, and of your probable daily mileage. On a first trip I would be inclined to assume that twenty or at most twenty-five miles would be a good day's run. With experience, you will find that anything up to fifty miles or even more is within your range. (My own average for the routes cycled was probably about thirty miles in a fullish day, though in some cases I did quite a bit more.)

The next step, of course, is to make a list of B and Bs in the relevant towns and villages. You then have two choices: to book ahead before you set off, or to leave it to the day itself, when you have a clear idea of exactly where you will be at nightfall. Leaving it till later does give you more flexibility – you can cut short the day to go for a stroll, or lengthen it out if you have a following wind and want to get some miles in. Outside the high season it will generally be safe to wait until mid-afternoon before trying to book, especially if you have some alternative addresses should your first choice be full. In the high season (weekends from May to the end of September, Easter, and all of July and August), it would be rash to leave things that late, and your peace of mind will benefit if you book all your accommodation a few days in advance.

Camping

The third alternative is to camp. This has some obvious drawbacks and if you have never camped or cycled, I would concentrate on enjoying the bicycle before wondering about tents. Camping commits you to carrying quite a lot of equipment, especially since you cannot rely on finding suitable official sites and so need to take a large water container, filled towards evening, for 'wild camping'. Camping loses its charm in bad weather: if you get a wet night after a wet day, a B and B's roof is nicer over your head than a layer of nylon. The lack of pleasant official sites, the fact that these are usually situated on main roads, and the difficulty of finding suitable alternatives can make it all seem a hassle.

All the same, I love camping, and as you read on you will discover that I camped on most of the expeditions recorded here. At Wells (Route 1) I used the council site, and there are a few other suitable official and commercial sites on or near the routes (in Sussex, details of sites near the South Downs Way will be found in any of the several guidebooks devoted to the Way). Elsewhere I asked farmers for permission to use a field or pitched my tent unobtrusively in the verges of quiet lanes and public paths and bridleways. The legality of this is doubtful, I suppose, but it is not always possible to find the landowner, and providing you do no damage and leave no rubbish you are not harming anyone.

Once you become adept at finding suitable places, camping is very flexible. It is also cheap, and it gets you into the deepest countryside.

If you enjoy camping, or think you might, by all means take a tent on your bike. I wish you luck, and think you will be as pleasantly surprised as I was by the secluded and silent pitches it is possible to find within the crowded counties near London, as well as in more peaceful Norfolk and Suffolk.

Places of Interest

Many a guidebook and itinerary has been constructed on the principle of linking together a chain of 'places of interest' – country houses, museums, theme parks, leisure centres. Plenty of what is nowadays called 'heritage' is there to be seen in south-east England and East Anglia, and much of it is indeed interesting or beautiful or both. None the less, the 'places of interest' format is not well suited to a cycling guidebook. The 'places' are often crowded, whereas cyclists tend to be looking for peace and quiet; and they are often on main roads, whereas cyclists may prefer lanes and byways.

My own criteria, in devising and riding these routes, were two. I was looking for attractive and varied landscapes, and for genuinely quiet, safe roads. Use of A roads is kept to an absolute minimum (less than ten miles in the whole book, apart from the coastal rides in Route 1, to which easily followed alternatives on the lanes are given), and even B roads are very largely avoided.

Two 'places of interest', Blythburgh church (Route 4) and the ruins of Bayham Abbey (Route 6), figured in my plans from the outset, but in general I tended to look out for attractive or historic sites as I rode rather than to allow their location to determine or even modify my itineraries.

In consequence, these rides often pass quite close to country houses, museums and famous gardens without actually visiting them. In such cases, your attention is drawn to the proximity of these places and suggestions are made as to how you might detour to see them. Usually this is done in the preliminary summary of the route (examples include Sissinghurst in Route 6 and Petworth House and Park in Route 12). If you want fuller information about historic houses and so on in the regions the routes pass through, standard gazetteers and guidebooks and Tourist Board publications will help you complete the picture.

This is a personal guide, focussed above all on landscape. However, in trying to convey a sense of the countryside and of the environment in general, I have given some account of the more modest and lesser-known buildings which I stopped and looked at and enjoyed.

The Routes in this Book

The routes that you will find in the following chapters are one rider's choice of one-, two- and three-day excursions in the country between London and the sea. There is a

chapter to each of the counties I visited (Essex I
reluctantly excluded as even the minor roads and lanes are
uncomfortably busy).

I claim to offer no more than an introduction to cycling
in Norfolk and Suffolk. Here, as elsewhere, the routes were
carefully chosen to cover varied terrain and avoid classified
roads. They were a pleasure to ride. I hope you too will
find the routes rewarding, and that my accounts of them
will inspire you both to ride where I rode and to explore
further this quiet, scenic region for yourselves. There is
clearly more to see, and more quiet lanes to see it from,
than these routes cover. East Anglia is very accessible from
London and from further afield, and I was surprised not to
see more cyclists there.

I would make larger claims for the routes in Kent and
Sussex. These are crowded, busy counties, and finding
extensive quiet rides is far from easy. I drew on many
years' experience to devise routes that followed safe roads
through landscapes at once characteristic, continuously
attractive and varied. In due course you may want to
modify the routes and make explorations of your own, but
you might well begin by following these eight rides exactly:
they are all delightful, and between them give a fine sense
of what Kent and Sussex have to offer the cyclist.

Each route is given in the same format and it will help
you make the most of this book if I briefly run through the
pattern that they follow.

At the start of each is a brief summary, outlining the
main landscape features and generally including
suggestions and information of a more practical kind: notes
on transport or accommodation, possible extensions or
modifications of the route, places of interest you will pass
nearby. These introductory sections will help you decide
which routes you are most interested in and would like to

investigate further.

This summary is followed by a more technical section, the heart of the route when it comes to actually setting out. There is a note of the distance – as accurate as care could make it, but translating map measurements into on-the-road miles is notoriously difficult, and an error of up to ten per cent either way is possible. Next is the number(s) of the relevant OS (Ordnance Survey) 1:50 000 sheet(s). These maps are in my view by far the best choice for cycling in the complex lanes and byways of southern England: smaller scales simply do not give enough detail, whereas larger-scale maps, informative as they are, cover too little ground per sheet. As you will see below, the OS 1:50 000 is indispensable when you come to follow the routes on the ground. The sketch maps accompanying the descriptions of the routes are a great help in visualising the overall shape of the ride, but the scale practicable in this book does not allow depiction of the detail needed to find your way. Some further notes on using maps are given below.

Next comes a note of the duration of the trip. This tells you how long it took me, but you may want to allow more (or less) time, depending how far you think you will ride each day and how much sightseeing, strolling, picnicking and taking it easy you like to fit in. My stated times do not allow for an overnight stay at the beginning or end of the routes, but this would give you a more relaxed, and longer, break, and may be essential if you have to make a long journey to reach the start and get home again.

A brief note about the terrain follows. This is simply to alert you to challenges and problems: hills, prevailing winds, stretches of main road (wherever the route includes any), and also stretches of unsurfaced tracks and bridleways on which you may have to push (though an

ATB will manage most of them) and which will be difficult
or impassable, often, in winter. In the case of both main
roads and unsurfaced tracks, your attention is drawn to
alternative routes which avoid these problematic stretches,
except in the very few cases where no practicable
alternative exists.

Finally comes the detailed itinerary – not very readable
prose (the itineraries were no great fun to write out either),
but the key to this book's practical uses. (See the section
below, *Itineraries and Maps*, for detailed advice on how to
follow these itineraries.)

The third and longest section is an extended personal
account of what I did and saw as I rode, alone and with
friends. These sections were a pleasure to write and they
are meant to be enjoyable reading. They will give you a
very detailed picture of the landscapes and other features
that you will encounter as you ride. But of course they can
only be an evocation: reading is one thing, riding is
another. I hope they will whet your appetite.

Choosing Your Route

Choosing the right route for a particular tour involves
decisions both aesthetic (what kind of landscape do you
want to visit?) and practical (how long do you want to be
away, how far do you want to travel to the tour's start,
does the ride involve climbs or distances you are not ready
to tackle?). The route texts cover all these questions, and
experienced cyclists can pick and choose from the twelve
routes according to taste and circumstances.

If you are new to cycle-touring, you would be well
advised to start with a gentle introduction. Your first trip
should be short, accessible and not too demanding. For

many readers, a day trip in the country south of London
will fit the bill. In terms of this book, Route 8, or (better)
the first part of it, as far as Fletching and back, is an ideal
choice. The out-and-back trip over flat Pevensey Levels at
the start of Route 10 is an even gentler ride, but the
landscape is less varied and Polegate is further than Lewes
from London.

A day trip in Sussex is not a practical option if you
come from the far side of the capital, as the effort of the
journey will hardly be repaid by just a few hours' cycling.
The Norfolk and Suffolk rides, which in terms of their
terrain are the easiest in the book, will make a good
introductory tour of two or three days each. Relatively
inexperienced riders from London and the south-east will
find that these East Anglian routes make an ideal next step
after one or two shorter expeditions nearer home.

The rest of the routes all include hilly sections, for the
simple reason that some of the loveliest country in Kent
and Sussex is to be found in the hills. The two delightful
day trips in the Kent and East Sussex Weald (Routes 6
and 9) will introduce you to the pains and very real
pleasures of upland riding, and convince you that the hard
work of climbing is well rewarded by the serenity and the
fine views you enjoy. Route 6 combines Wealden hills with
lower-lying orchards, while Route 9 is almost entirely up-
and-down. The remaining Kent and Sussex rides, all two-
day trips, combine stretches in the Weald and the Downs
with flatter going in the river valleys and plains.

Avoiding major roads as they do, all the routes will be
passably quiet even in the height of summer. Those which
skirt the sea (Routes 1, 3, 4, 5 and 10) are, however,
likely to be noticeably more tranquil out of season.
Wherever you ride you will have a more peaceful time if
you go outside July and August, and in summer especially

it makes sense to avoid weekends (if you are lucky enough to be able to get time off during the week).

Most of these rides were in fact made on weekdays between September and June. If the weather is fine, May and June are wonderful months for cycling. The southern English landscape is at its best, with trees and flowers and cottage gardens headily burgeoning, and you have long, light evenings to enjoy.

Itineraries and Maps

Having chosen your route and acquired the necessary map(s) (Ordnance Survey maps of all these southern counties should be available in good bookshops nationwide, but see the Appendix for help if you cannot obtain them), you need to turn to the detailed itinerary and trace it out on the map. Use a soft pencil, 2B or softer: it leaves a good visible mark, will not damage the paper, and can easily be erased after you have ridden the route.

In preparing the itineraries, I took the view that too much information is preferable to too little. Compass bearing, place-names, grid references, numbers of classified roads and instructions as to whether to turn right or left or keep straight on at junctions are all used to provide a very detailed text which should translate onto the map without ambiguity or prolonged head-scratching by you, the reader. I have not, however, given instructions regarding every single lane junction; where circumstances allow, I have given such general guidance as 'take lanes NW and then N via Fring, Sedgeford and Ringstead to Holme next the Sea' (Route 1). Anyone looking at the map will at once identify the route to be taken.

If you are not used to decoding grid references you will need some practice before it comes easily (instructions are given on the OS maps themselves as to how to do it). Grid references are a helpful additional source of orientation for both compiler and user of the itineraries, and in some cases, where a lane junction is some way from any named place, it is only by means of a grid reference that it can be securely identified.

Your bike serviced, your kit packed, and your OS map marked up from the itineraries, how will you fare when you set off into the lanes? However clearly you have marked the map, will you be able to follow it on the ground?

Again, practice, and patience, will help you overcome any initial difficulty. Even the most experienced route-finders sometimes go astray in complex lanes. Remember you are in England, not Antarctica: soon enough you will come to a named settlement – and nothing is going to eat or freeze you in the meantime! Use a compass if you find it helpful, learn to absorb all the information that the maps provide (contours, churches, tree types, streams and rivers) as a supplement to lanes and signposts, and develop the habit of checking your general direction by reference to the sun's position. A cyclist following metalled lanes through inhabited country faces few of the map-reading problems met, and successfully overcome, by walkers on pathless moors. Careful use of the map will soon become second nature and once you have had some experience, you will rarely, if ever, miss the way.

The narrow lanes which the routes given here mostly follow are a far cry from broad highways with massive, obtrusive direction signs and road markings. Plunging into their leafy light and shade, staying for hours in quiet

country with only the whirr of the bike and the song of
birds to listen to much of the time – this is another world.
It is a little disorientating at first, maybe, but exhilarating
from the start and, before long, enchanting.

4. Norfolk

Norfolk, they say, is flat. But a glance at the map shows that little of the county has the mathematical flatness of reclaimed land, such as you find in the level fens and marshes of Cambridgeshire and Lincolnshire. 'High Norfolk', the region north-west of Norwich which I explored and very much enjoyed, is pleasantly rolling. The open plateau never reaches any great height, but its long views and breezy spaciousness put me in mind of the bare downland of Wiltshire and Hampshire.

It is true that Norfolk has no long, steep hills: good news for less experienced and energetic riders. This is quiet country, too, where it is not so hard to get away and stay away from traffic. At the time of the Domesday Book, Norfolk was England's most populous county, and it prospered for centuries as an exporter of wool and, later, of finished cloth. However, the Industrial Revolution passed it by, for it lacked the raw materials which attracted the new factories and factory towns. It has built on its farming tradition, and retains a markedly agricultural economy. There is little heavy industry, and the towns are small. Local traffic is accordingly light, though summer visitors increase the volume of cars, especially near the Broads and the sea coast.

Relatively uncrowded and undeveloped, the county presents the cyclist with a wealth of choice and a welcome absence of problems. The routes described in this chapter

(I cycled them in succession over four days, but here they
are divided into two separate trips, lasting two and a half
and one and a half days, respectively) represent just one
sample of what Norfolk has to offer.

No one should miss visiting the superb coast between
Hunstanton and Blakeney, distinguished both in its
scenery and in its plant and animal life. Norfolk naturalists
were among the earliest to perceive the urgency of
conserving natural habitats (the Norfolk and Norwich
Naturalists' Society was founded in 1869, and the Norfolk
Naturalists' Trust in 1926; together with the Nature
Conservancy Council they manage an extensive range of
nature reserves): today's unspoiled coastal scenery owes
much to their pioneering efforts. I explored no further east
than Cley, but dunes and sands run all the way round to
Great Yarmouth. In many places there is access to the
coast by paths and tracks, but not by metalled roads. Even
in summer, I imagine that many of these beaches must be
uncrowded.

Inland lie the Broads. Lanes run down to some of them,
though none follows the waterside for long (and there are
few footpaths). Many cyclists will want to have a look at
these famous lakes, busy though they are in summer with
waterborne tourists.

Another distinctive Norfolk habitat is Breckland, centred
on Thetford. Unfortunately, the open heaths which once
stretched for miles have shrunk and shrunk under the joint
impact of modern agriculture, large-scale forestry and the
military. Much of Breckland now consists either of what
the compilers of one guide call 'dense forestry plantations
. . . dull going', or of battle-training areas. There are also a
number of RAF and USAF airfields. This, indeed, is one
of the areas whose despoliation by the Ministry of Defence

W G Hoskins deplores in his classic account, *The Making of the English Landscape*. If (like me) you decide that Breckland is not for you, you can console yourself with the reflection that much common land, often of considerable ecological interest, survives in scattered patches throughout Norfolk. This is on a small scale: one understands why an officer of the East Anglian Nature Conservancy Council regretted, twenty-five years ago, that 'we no longer have the wonderful open views over miles of rolling heathland – "wild Breckland" as it was once called has gone for ever.' But the surviving heaths and commons, unkempt, overgrown with silvery shrubs, make a pleasant contrast to the tidily ploughed autumn fields as you explore the Wensum and Nar valleys.

In Norfolk, as everywhere in lowland England, the character of the farming is a predominant influence on the character of the landscape. I loved 'High Norfolk' – though here, too, one must record the disappearance of an earlier and more natural scene. During the late eighteenth and earlier nineteenth centuries, these light, sandy soils (as you move east, the land grows heavier) were transformed from what Arthur Young, the agriculturist and topographical writer, called 'rabbit and rye country'. The underlying marl was mixed with the topsoil, which was manured by pasturing sheep. Then came the famous 'Norfolk rotation', in which cereals alternated with roots and clover. 'Turnip' Townshend and Coke of Holkham (I visited the estate in the first of the two routes) are famous names from this improving age.

Nowadays, sugar beet is much grown alongside barley and wheat, and carrots, celery and other horticultural crops are grown, too. Chemical fertiliser is of course used on an unprecedented scale – to the detriment of the notoriously nitrate-rich East Anglian water supply. But the land still delights the eye with its clean, open lines.

Parliamentary enclosure had a great impact here. One mark of this lies in the many straight lanes, with noticeably wide grass verges. The whole aspect of this north-western landscape, in its distinction from other parts of the county, has to do with this different history. Discussing the effects of enclosure in East Anglia, W G Hoskins writes:

> Even if one had never visited this part of England, the map would suggest that there are fundamental differences in the way in which the landscape of the two halves of the counties had evolved. This is particularly striking in Norfolk. In the east and centre of the county we find a close network of narrow, winding lanes, wandering from hamlet to hamlet and farm to farm. . . . It is a closely-packed map with hardly a straight line or an empty space in it. The west of the county is entirely different, even to the casual glance of a motorist: far fewer lanes and by-ways, more villages, straighter roads, large empty spaces between the villages, the whole landscape or map more 'open' altogether.

This spaciousness struck me particularly after Holt on my first ride, and before the intriguingly named village of Stratton Strawless on my second.

Having enjoyed this fine open country – and with a cyclist's less 'casual' eye and more sensitive awareness of gradient and topography – I hope now to return to visit the country south of Norwich: the drained levels behind Breydon Water by Yarmouth, the twisting lanes along the water-meadows of the lower Yare, and the valleys of the Waveney and the Little Ouse which mark the border between Norfolk and Suffolk.

Accommodation is particularly plentiful along the coast, and with some forethought can readily be found inland. Norfolk is quite well supplied with campsites, too. It also offers better opportunities for 'wild camping' than most of southern England. There are those wide, quiet verges, and once the corn is harvested you can ask a farmer for permission to use a stubble field. But you will not be able to put up a tent in the protected coastal areas: here, conservation must have priority, and you will need to stick to the official sites.

Trains run to Norwich from London Liverpool Street, and to King's Lynn from Liverpool Street and King's Cross. Connections from the Midlands and the North are via Peterborough and Ely. Beyond Norwich, local trains run to Cromer and Yarmouth, as well as down to Ipswich.

Norfolk is close enough to London to make a two- or three-day trip worthwhile, but it also lends itself – alone or with Suffolk – to more extended touring. Remember, these routes are no more than a sample. A strategically placed bed and breakfast or self-catering cottage would make a base for a week of day trips. And it would be easy to follow all or part of the routes given here and then link them up, via one or two days' ride south, with the Suffolk rides in Chapter 5.

Route 1:
The North Norfolk Coast

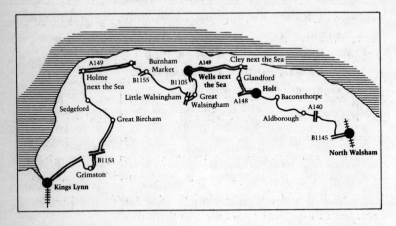

King's Lynn to North Walsham

From Hunstanton east as far as Cley and beyond, North
Norfolk meets the sea in a coast of rare beauty – and rare
interest for naturalists and ornithologists. It is the home of
a colony of seals, and its salt marshes, among the most
extensive in Europe, are the breeding-ground of many
kinds of seabird. Partly because building has always been
difficult on this marshy and unstable terrain, and partly
because most of the coastline is now protected and
conserved, the shore remains remarkably unspoiled. At
Wells next the Sea, the busiest of the smaller resorts, you
have only to walk half a mile or so along the beach to find
yourself alone in an expanse of flat sand, backed by high
pine-clad dunes.

Walkers on the Norfolk Coast Path, a designated Long
Distance Path, must enjoy many lonely miles where they
share the sand-flats, dunes, marshes and shingle banks

only with the birds. The path, with its tracts of sand and soft mud, is not negotiable by bicycle (or mountain bike). To enjoy the solitude and desolation of the beaches, you will need to leave your machine and walk at least a few hundred yards: the OS map shows a number of dead-end tracks that give access to the seashore.

Back on the bike, be sure to ride some way along the coast road, with its views over the low-lying foreshore to dunes and sands and open sea. In winter, I was assured, this road is quiet. It owes its status as an A road to its obvious usefulness to tourists – so you must get up early if you are to enjoy riding on it in the summer months. It can hardly be safe, let alone pleasant, in the middle of the day in the high season, and alternatives are given for the two stretches of my journey where I followed it.

Inland, you will notice the dry red soil. The lane edges are full of powdery sand, mixed sometimes with shingle and looking almost as if it had blown in from the sea. The terrain, never absolutely flat but never really hilly, varies all along the pleasant hinterland. Variety comes from the short pastoral river valleys that intersect the plateau, from the subtle differences between one expanse of open country and the next, from the copses and small woods which adorn the horizon (but which must have an altogether bleaker character from November to May, for they are all deciduous), and from the movement of clouds against the brilliant sky for which Norfolk is celebrated.

King's Lynn to North Walsham

Distance: approx. 90 miles. OS 132, 133

Duration: Two overnight stays. One short afternoon, two full days

Terrain: Gently rolling, flat near coast. Onshore winds can be strong and persistent, especially near the sea. *NB: stretches of this route follow the A149 coast road*, pleasant only out of season or in early morning. Alternatives are suggested to these stretches in the itinerary.

Itinerary: Train to **King's Lynn** (from London Liverpool Street or King's Cross, via Cambridge; from the Midlands and the North, via Peterborough and Ely).

Leave King's Lynn on the A1078/A148 and continue on the A148 just past roundabout junction with the A149. Fork right on lane to Grimston, where take the B1153 left, via short stretch of A148, and back on the B1153 to Great Bircham. Take lanes NW and then N via Fring, Sedgeford and Ringstead to **Holme next the Sea** (25 miles).

Take the A149 via Thornham, Brancaster and Brancaster Staithe to Burnham Deepdale. Fork right on lane and via short stretch of B1155 to **Burnham Market** (alternatively, from Holme return to Ringstead and take lane almost due E to Burnham Market) (35 miles).

Take lane SE via Burnham Thorpe to New Holkham park gate (grid ref. 882397). Ride to and from Obelisk, then under Triumphal Arch to lane crossroads, where take E to crossroads at grid ref. 904395. Turn S, fork left, and join the B1105 to ride S into Little Walsingham. Leave on the B1388 and take lane left at Great Walsingham to ride via Wighton and the B1105 to **Wells next the Sea** (54 miles).

Take coast road E to Blakeney and Cley next the Sea (alternatively, ride SE inland, on the B1105, lanes, and the B1388, and join coast road only for short stretch between Blakeney and Cley). From Cley, ride S on lanes on E bank of Glaven and cross river to the B1156 at Glandford, riding SSE and via short stretch of A148 to **Holt** (69 miles).

From Holt, take lane to Baconsthorpe (grid ref. 125372). Then on lanes via Plumstead and Matlaske (grid ref. 150349) to Aldborough, where cross Scarrow Beck (grid ref. 185337) and E on lanes crossing the A140 and almost to the A149 at Antingham. But turn right on lane just before main road, and left 2 miles south to enter **North Walsham** on the B1145 (90 miles).

North Walsham station has trains for Norwich, where there are connections for London Liverpool Street and to Ely and Peterborough.

My rail journey up to King's Lynn was my first trip to East Anglia for many years. Norwich I once knew well, but the Norfolk countryside would be a new experience. As the train swayed and rattled over the levels north of Cambridge, I looked for characteristics of this new landscape. Flatness, of course – indeed here, in the fen country round Ely, a flatness more absolute than I would find later. With nothing to divert it, the line ran with mathematical straightness over dark fen earth. Through the windows, on this afternoon of heat and bright light, came scents of autumn crops: a field of celery on the right, a field of drying onions on the left.

At Ely, I was held up. Engineering work meant that the line to Lynn was closed until four, and the replacement bus service could not take bikes. I strolled into the town – or city, I suppose, since its cathedral is what makes it famous: but it has a pleasant small-town atmosphere. Down by the Ouse, the boating season, and the lunchtime drinking in the sun season, were evidently far from over. The river was attractive, if a little crowded (painted barges, smart motor launches, an eight putting out to row), the pub terrace overlooked the water, and a glass of cool Norwich bitter seemed the right way to prepare for a visit to the cathedral.

From the riverside I walked up through a pastoral park, with cows grazing in an adjoining field, into the precincts. Chichester, Canterbury, Norwich, Ely, Lincoln: Ely must be the quietest of these cathedral cities. The church was being much restored, and the medieval Lady Chapel, the largest in England, was closed. But I enjoyed the celebrated Octagon, the colonnaded tower which lets daylight into the heart of the building. Dating from the early fourteenth century, it is almost as remarkable for its technological assurance as for its aesthetic grace.

I arrived at King's Lynn for the afternoon rush hour, and there was nose-to-tail traffic all the way out to the roundabout. The town is not large, and fairly out of the way, but it is obviously the local employment centre. Down by the small port on the river, I had peered into the yard of a canning factory. A great hopper stood full of what looked like peas (though September seemed late for peas). The OS map shows a large sugar factory, visible from the train. There must be services, too: schools, hospitals, the banks and lawyers' offices that occupy the buildings around the old square near the waterfront, as they occupy historic parts of so many English towns. For all that, I was taken aback by the volume of traffic. Leaving the A road and taking the wide lane to Grimston, I was still among cars. Here I rode across a tract of heathland typical, I imagine, of the Breckland district a little further south-east. Birches and small oaks stood among the bracken, with a blaze of heather in the background, and the newly ploughed sandy fields ran in among the heath.

The agricultural character of North Norfolk began to reveal itself as I took the quiet B road through Flitcham towards Bircham, climbing steadily onto a plateau of open fields and low thorn hedges. Roadside fields often had neither hedge nor fence, and this accentuated the open aspect of the landscape. The farming is almost all arable – grain and beet – so barriers to keep livestock in are not needed (though I did see occasional black-faced sheep, and one field of pigs, each with its own shiny metal hutch).

Halfway between Flitcham and Great Bircham the road is crossed by the Peddar's Way, a designated Long Distance Path which strikes north towards the coast and which I had decided to follow for some miles should it prove passable. It lies on an old Roman route, probably a military road and possibly a means of access to a point near Hunstanton from where the Wash could be crossed. In places the Peddar's Way runs along tracks and made roads, in others it is no more than a path across fields. Here, where it traverses the B1153, the OS map depicts it as an 'other road, drive or track': it is uncoloured on the map, whereas surfaced lanes are yellow. It is notoriously hard to anticipate what kind of going these 'other roads' will offer. As a rule they will at least allow you to push your bike (which is by no means always true of bridle paths), but they will not necessarily allow you to ride. In the present case, the path was no more than a rather overgrown sandy track. Not even a mountain bike could have coped with it hereabouts. I walked a few yards to the north, scaring two rabbits and a stoat. The path looked little used, though it must offer constantly pleasant, if rarely dramatic, walking.

Riding on, I dropped into Fring: the first quiet lane I had taken, and very attractive, especially as it curves into the valley bottom past a copse. In the village, I asked a man in a garden to fill my water bottle. The water tasted good, he told me: it was 'Fring water' (I had passed another borehole, too, back in Bircham), but there was too much nitrate in it. And yes, this was a quiet spot and a quiet road, except at summer weekends when those who knew the way used it as a short cut back from the sea, roaring through the narrow lanes.

Beyond Fring, I was more and more aware of another aspect of these lanes (and indeed, as it proved, of many

Norfolk lanes): their wide verges, often eight feet broad
and more. This too adds to the landscape's openness,
especially as the verges are without ditches, an indication
of how dry the climate is. For me, these wide, well-tended
verges had also an immediate practical significance:
wherever the lanes were quiet (as they were just here), the
verges would offer an ideal place to put up a tent. Between
Fring and Sedgeford, where the road runs alongside an
open stubblefield, I stopped, put up my tent, and lit my
stove. In the dusk, a score or so of pheasants scurried and
scratched in the stubble, and a hare burst from the copse
that edged the field.

Next morning, I woke – with the pheasants, which
included two or three of the bright-hued Lady Amherst's
variety – to a soft grey dawn and an easterly breeze: the
clear hot weather of the last weeks was about to change. I
lit a fire and boiled my kettle, pleased to note that the few
drivers passing at this early hour seemed friendly and glad
enough to see me. Then I set off for the coast, impatient to
discover its scenery. It was impossible to hurry the
journey, however, for the valley between Fring and
Sedgeford was delightful, its intimate scale and green
leaves contrasting with the pale colours and long
perspectives of the higher ground. I rode past parkland, a
Montessori school, the yard of a supplier of beekeeping
equipment (where dozens of empty hives stood stacked), a
field of white ducks who had nibbled the grass to a fine
short turf on which feeding-racks full of fresh straw stood
for them to pick at. Then on to Ringstead:

Ringstead Church, 9.45 am, 8 September 1989
Sitting on bench by water tap – square tower of this flint church
has been repaired in brick. Heterogeneous building materials

much used, in one and the same building, locally: flint, chalk rubble, sandy limestone rubble, brick. But all the rooves have red tiles. I can see the red rooves of Ringstead village, tall trees (oak and horse chestnut) framing them. Then beyond, a typical plateau landscape: large open stubblefields, low thorn hedges. In the middle distance, to the left, stubble burners are at work. Horizon: a fine line of old trees.

And so to Holme. Out of Ringstead, you climb – every little slope counts in this low-lying country – to a hundred feet or so. Dropping towards the coast, you have a long view of the North Sea, spread wide at the end of your narrow lane. I saw it dark blue, with white crests just beginning to build up in the breeze. Out on the beach, with low chalk cliffs to the west and the salt marshes and sandbanks of the nature reserve to the east, I sat and drank coffee from my flask and watched a group of riders gallop their horses across the firm sands left by the ebbing tide. The place could not be called remote: to get there, I had crossed golf links, with a notice warning me to beware of flying golfballs. But to someone used (as I am) to the sea in Sussex, where almost every accessible beach is developed and where houses straggle virtually the entire length of the shore, this landscape and seascape were beautifully unspoiled.

Along the coast road, getting busier but still pleasant, were pubs, seafood shops, bed and breakfasts, antique shops and art galleries . . . but not in such density as to dominate one's recollection. On the contrary, what I remember is the compactness of the coastal villages, the open land between the road and the salt marshes (with orchards in several places, rather to my surprise, for the sea wind can be bitter), and the views.

Back inland, my route passed through Burnham Thorpe, Holkham Park and Walsingham. Many of these Norfolk

villages have a three-dimensional wooden signboard set up
on the green, and at Burnham Thorpe (where there are
pleasant playing fields and fine terraced cottages) the
emblems include the Red Ensign and the Union Jack. This
is in homage to Horatio Nelson, born at Burnham and
commemorated in the name of many local pubs.

Beyond the village, the road dips into a hollow where no
trees can be seen, and you get a brief sense of how bleak
this landscape would be without the softening shape and
colour of the copses. Climbing to Holkham, you reach fine
timber. The demesne is edged all around with mature
beech and oak. Inside – the grounds are open to the public
during the day – lies one of those English parklands whose
serenity and good taste are inseparably bound up with
privilege and exclusiveness. The Earls of Leicester live at
Holkham, in a Palladian mansion whose façade, across
velvety lawns and tediously geometrical flowerbeds, you
will see if you ride the mile or so from the park gate up
the tree-lined avenue to the Obelisk. Just inside the park is
Longlands Farm, presumably worked by tenants of the
estate, and itself an antique and formal building, with
stables like cloisters and an ornamental clocktower.

Further on, as you follow a wide-verged lane towards
the B1105 and Little Walsingham, you should look out for
another fine group of buildings at Edgar Farm. There is an
impressive and beautifully maintained cluster of red-roofed
barns. The farmhouse stands a little apart, with darker
tiles and a large flint-walled kitchen garden. The flint
walling is repeated in an adjoining terrace of labourers'
cottages, one more example of the sturdiness and fine
proportions which, I was beginning to realise, distinguish
the vernacular architecture of this part of Norfolk.

I knew I would be out of sympathy with Walsingham's
famous shrine, with its heavily High Church atmosphere.

What was it that made up that cultural moment of the 1930s, when this ancient pilgrimage station was renovated and reopened (the shrine was originally founded in 1061, and was destroyed in the Reformation in 1538)? You catch something of the mood in T S Eliot's writing – its best and most intense side in the *Four Quartets*, I suppose. But Walsingham, for all its ecumenical flavour, evoked for me only an echo of meaningless, immemorial and sometimes bloody theological dispute. . . . I turned away, spiritually and literally, and thought as I rode along the upper Stiffkey valley of some lines from *East Coker*, my memory stirred, no doubt, by the morning's sea views:

> Dawn points, and another day
> Prepares for heat and silence. Out at sea the dawn wind
> Wrinkles and slides.

But the weather was not like that now. Swallows were flitting restlessly across the water-meadows, where I saw the first dairy herd of my trip so far. The sky was grey, and I was in for a windy night at Wells.

So windy, in fact, that I barely slept. The District Council campsite is well laid out, spacious and friendly, but it is in a terribly exposed position, out at the harbour mouth near the Lifeboat Station, and its loose sandy soil is poor anchorage for tentpegs. Every twenty minutes from half past ten at night until six in the morning, I would crawl from my sleeping bag into the gale and the dark, and try once more to jam the pegs into the ground . . . to lie listening disconsolately, afterwards, as they were ripped out one after another, until the beating of loose guys against the tent grew too irritating to bear and I would crawl out once more. Not long after first light, a friendly family from Birmingham, watching me load my bike for an early and welcome departure, invited me into their all-mod-cons tent, where the kettle stood singing on the gas stove, and gave me a large mug of hot tea. Let me repeat here the warm thanks I gave them at the time. They hadn't slept a wink either, they said, with the constant gusts shaking their frame tent all night long.

All the same, Wells is a nice place. Like Blakeney and Cley further along the coast, it retains, beneath its summer veneer of tourism (the Burger Bar whose green neon light glows at you through the dusk as you walk in along the creek, the arcade full of slot machines and video games), another, older and more romantic identity: the identity of a seaport and fishing harbour. In the sixteenth century, Wells was Norfolk's chief port. The only boat moored there when I visited was a dredger, but I noticed a recently completed silo/warehouse at the quayside for the loading of animal feedstuffs, which I suppose are produced and milled locally. A few yards in from the gaudy waterfront, where the narrow streets shelter you from the wind and you at once feel warmer and more protected, there are houses which must date from no later than the early nineteenth century. Here, in Staithe Street and High Street, you again feel the presence of something more deeply rooted than tourism.

Nevertheless, it was as a tourist that I went there, drawn by the beach. The dunes, planted in Victorian times with Corsican pines, run for miles, and you can wander freely among them (they belong to the Holkham estate, however) as well as on the sands, which at low tide are of considerable extent. They cover quickly once the tide flows, and large warning notices exhort you not to get trapped on the offshore banks and shoals. This fine coast has a perilous and even sinister side: quicksands, strong currents, constant erosion (some areas of the dunes are fenced off to protect the grass which holds the shifting sands together), and storms and freak tides. Like the Dutch coast opposite, it is vulnerable when the water rises high. In Wells, which suffered badly, a mark on the newly built sea defences shows the level reached by the disastrous flood of 1953.

I rode east on the empty road as far as Stiffkey, my sleepless night having made an early start possible:

By Stiffkey church, 8.00 am, 9 September 1989
Stiffkey – sitting against the churchyard wall drinking coffee (brewed out of the wind in campsite washroom). What a lovely village – green, where the river flows – and how carefully the old houses, terraces too, have been restored.

Road from Wells: very agricultural. Odd glimpses of the sea. A number of tracks 'Unsuitable for Motors' run down to the shore: with campable verges, too.

Wells: sea, dunes. Nature reserve: no fires, no stoves, no camping. WARNING about being cut off. Also about dead seals infected with canine distemper. Low tide. Then as tide came in, evening fell, wind got up, lights came on bobbing in the channel. Clack-clack-clack of rigging on rocked, windblown moored yachts. Rising water lifts them off black, rather smelly mud. Beach huts on stilts. 1953 floodmark. Memorial – anchor sculpture – to lifeboat crew drowned last century.

At Blakeney and at Cley, you will find the same maritime atmosphere. Offshore is the long shingle spit of Blakeney Point, with boat-trips from Blakeney and Morston which include a view of the seal colony.

After Cley, I turned back inland. The coast road was getting busier, and the best of the coast was past. High points of my inland ride were the crossing of the Glaven, where ducks swam up in dozens, expecting food, as I wheeled my bike across the wooden footbridge; the pretty ornamental waters the river makes as it flows through Bayfield Hall, just upstream; and then the long, drifting ride beyond Holt. Here the plateau had an especially airy and open feel, even though soft drizzling cloud blurred the distance, and here the little agricultural villages – Baconsthorpe, Plumstead, Matlaske – seemed particularly lost, self-contained, rural. It hardly felt like south-east England at all. It felt, anyway, like an earlier, quieter time.

Route 2:
Norfolk Rivers – The Wensum and the Nar

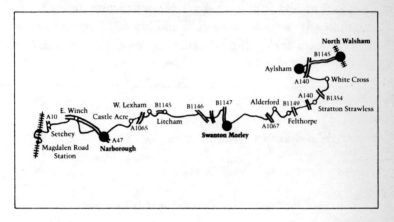

North Walsham to King's Lynn

Even apart from the Broads, Norfolk has a number of rivers that look tempting on the map. In the south, the Waveney marks the border with Suffolk. Norwich is at the confluence of the Wensum, the Yare and the Tas, and west of Norwich you will find the Little Ouse and its tributaries, the Thet and the Black Bourn.

I rode up one river flowing east, the Wensum, and down another, the Nar, that flows west to King's Lynn. Combined with the previous route (Route 1), this makes a round trip from Lynn, an easy ride of four or five days. Taken on its own – it can easily be joined near the start from Norwich, incidentally, via the A140 and B1140 – it would make an ideal short summer break, at a time when the coast and the Broads are uncomfortably crowded. The little lanes I followed might have some tourist traffic in the high season, but I doubt that this ever amounts to much.

Certainly when I was there the second weekend of
September, I found very quiet riding – and scenic riding
much of the way. Between Alderford and Narborough,
there is delightful country and surprising variety: glimpses
of parkland and ornamental waters, small hilly fields by
the upper Wensum, the elegant solidity of Litcham (whose
church offers some off-the-beaten-track sightseeing), and
the rural seclusion of Fiddler's Green.

North Walsham to King's Lynn

Distance: approx. 75 miles. OS 133, 132

Duration: One overnight stay. Two moderately easy days

Terrain: Mostly flat, all easy. There are some fairly exposed
stretches, but you will have the east wind behind you!

Itinerary: Train via Norwich (from London Liverpool Street or via
Peterborough and Ely) to **North Walsham**.
  From North Walsham, take the B1145 to cross the A140 and
enter Aylsham on lanes. Continue on lanes to Burgh next Aylsham
(grid ref. 217252), then just E to White Cross, where you take the
lane that runs S. After this lane swings W, take first left, obliquely
under railway viaduct, across the B1354, and along western edge of
Buxton village. At grid ref. 230206, turn right on lane to Stratton
Strawless. Continue on lanes SW across the A140 and B1149 and to
Felthorpe (16 miles).
  Ride SW through lane crossroads to T-junction. Turn right and
follow lane to Alderford village and church, taking the left fork to
River Farm (grid ref. 108189). Cross the river, and the A1067, and
turn right on lanes, following S bank of Wensum through
Easthaugh, Lyng and Mill Street to Elsing (grid ref. 052166). Here
take lane W to **Swanton Morley** (31 miles).
  Ride N to river crossing (again called Mill Street), but take lane

left to follow riverbank round and back S by disused railway line towards Hoe. Do not enter Hoe, but turn right on lanes (at grid ref. 989168) and cross the B1110. At the B1146, turn right for less than 1 mile and then left on lanes via Gressenhall and just N of due W to **Litcham** (grid ref. 887177) (45 miles).

Take the B1145 W out of Litcham, and then fork left on lanes along N bank of the Nar to West Lexham. Cross the river on the lane, fork right, and cross the A1065 to take trackway and join lane W via Fiddler's Green to Castle Acre. Cross to S bank, fork right, and take right again to follow lane through South Acre, via Mill House (grid ref. 789150) and then SW to **Narborough** (57 miles).

Cross river Nar on the A47, and take lane left via Pentney to turning for Abbey Farm and ruins (grid ref. 702126). Here follow lane N via common to East Winch, on the A47, and take the main road left for less than 2 miles before forking left on lane to Blackborough End. Continue just S of W to Setchey, on the A10, which you must take S to the river crossing. Here follow the lane to the right, along the embankment. Cross railway and turn left down riverbank, following lane back E towards Watlington, but turning off right to **Magdalen Road station** (75 miles).

Magdalen Road station is the first stop on the line from King's Lynn to Ely and Cambridge (for Peterborough and London). If you wish to enter King's Lynn itself, it is 4 miles N of the route, on lanes, from the junction at grid ref. 611140.

Water, and attractively restored or carefully preserved old buildings near the water, are motifs of this ride. Entering Aylsham on lanes west of the main Norwich road, you pass through the oddly-named quarter of Dunkirk, where you will see lawns and a weir. A little further on, at Oxnead, beyond Burgh next Aylsham, there is a fine (and private) sweep of sward running back along the riverbank to the picturesque Hall. Here is that very English combination of elegance and exclusiveness: large-lettered placards reminding you that the fishing is Strictly Private and that you must Keep Out. You will see similar notices from time to time on the ride, especially as you cross the

Wensum between Great Witchingham Hall and Weston
Hall. Here, there is even a stretch of the river fenced off as
a private boating lake. At least it was being put to good
use when I passed: noisy children were paddling canoes in
the gentle current.

From Burgh over to the Wensum, you pass at first
through flattish arable land. It seemed dour the day I was
there, with grey skies and a wind strong enough to lift the
topsoil from recently harrowed fields and send it scurrying
in dusty clouds along the lanes. Turning towards Stratton
Strawless, and wondering what medieval thriftlessness had
earned the place its name, I heard irregular jangling from
the church: was it the wind, swinging the loosened bells in
the square flint tower? The vicarage stood nearby, with
slate rooftiles, unusual in this part of the world, giving it
an admonitory air. The village seemed mournful, like the
plateau shorn of its crops, waiting for winter. . . .
Remember, when you are cycling, that your depressed
mood may simply be the result of hunger. Just beyond
Stratton Strawless, I stopped and took out my flask of tea
and ate chunks of bread and bites of Edam cheese. The
mere beneath the bridge where I was sitting was muddy
and undistinguished (earlier in the year it would have been
colourful, with its masses of waterlilies in bloom), but still
my surroundings brightened as my stomach filled. Soon
the mystery of the bells – ringing, now, more rhythmically
and harmoniously, and more insistently – was solved: a
white Rolls Royce full of bridesmaids crossed the bridge,
followed by car after car of the wedding party on their way
to church.

A few miles further on, the Rolls passed me on its way
back, empty but for the chauffeur, who had taken off his
rather ludicrous livery jacket and was smoking a roll-up.
By now I was in the undistinguished woodland

sandwiched between the A140 and the A1067 as they fan
out north of Norwich. This is coniferous, with a bit of ash
and oak along the edges. Various small enterprises flourish
in gaps among the trees: a poultry farm, a garden centre, a
car-breaker's yard, the Norfolk Pet Crematorium

Once you reach the valley of the Wensum, more varied
and attractive landscapes begin. Beyond the parkland at
the river crossing comes a stretch of hilly fields, for above
Easthaugh and Lyng there is a drop of a hundred feet
from the plateau to the riverbed: almost mountainous, by
East Anglian standards. The reddish ploughlands, green
copses and occasional water-meadows and rougher
pastures are on a more intimate scale than the wide
upland grainfields. This is very quiet country, too: only an
occasional car passed. Near Elsing, by a bridge over the
Penny Spot beck, I found a perfect place to camp, a well-
sheltered clearing right beside the water. I had planned to
look for a B and B in Dereham; but now I stopped, leaned
my bike against the parapet, put up my tent, lit a small
fire in the moist grass of the verge, and set the kettle to
boil. Later, as dusk gathered, the copse behind me rang
with the sudden squawking cries of pheasants. Hunters
were out after them: a Landrover emerged from the
fieldgate at the top of the grass track next to me, and as it
turned into the lane I saw four trussed dead birds
swinging from the roof behind the driver's head. But I am
glad to say that no angler came to molest the fish – a
trout? – which I had seen poised against the current in a
pool below the bridge.

My fish was still there the following morning. The stream's
gurgling had lulled me into a long, sweet sleep: a welcome
restorative after my wakeful and windy night at Wells
(Route 1). I woke to a fresher day, with the sky showing

pale blue through rifts in the fleecy clouds.

At first I enjoyed more valley riding. Beyond Swanton Morley is a beautiful and secluded half hour's run between the river (a sizeable tributary, now, of the Wensum) and a disused railway. I rolled easily along in the shade of tall trees, with a narrow stubble strip to my left and to my right the quiet water-meadows where the sun caught the silvery backs of windblown willow-leaves. Then over the plateau to another river, the Nar, which I joined at Litcham.

Nothing on the map indicates that Litcham is worth going out of your way to see. Those of you who (like me) generally avoid 'places of interest', since in summer they tend to be magnets for crowds and cars, will know that often, in England, some unsung village will none the less offer a plain but memorable church, an old flint barn, a terrace of beautifully weathered brick: some curiosity of architecture or masonry which persuades you off your bike for a closer look. Drinking coffee at Litcham by the sign on the green, I admired the fine houses, built (I discovered) in the eighteenth century for the most part – in 1638, almost all the older buildings were lost in a fire. The church was spared (though its thatched roof probably perished), and is well worth a visit. An informative pamphlet will draw your attention to its exceptional features: the medieval piscina and rood screen, the fourteenth-century oak coffer of Flemish workmanship, the hexagonal pulpit 'bought in a London junk shop in 1890' but dating from the fifteenth century. You are bound to admire the delicate grace of the structure, too. The master builder responsible for Litcham church is thought to be one William Hindley, later in charge of work at Norwich and at York Minster.

Beyond Litcham is Lexham Hall, with ornamental

waters (dried, when I passed, to a thin silvery trickle) and a vineyard well sited on the sloping north bank of the Nar. After West Lexham, down a sandy but rideable track off the A1065, you will find the quintessential village green, a triangular lawn lying between lane and river and cropped by ducks and geese. If you have a camera and want to capture this rural moment, you may or may not be glad to hear that some of the ducks, when I rode past, were deplorably bedraggled, like kids with hair and jackets especially rumpled for the school photo: perfectly groomed ducks might make the scene too much of a cliché. Fiddler's Green, Broadmeadow Common (like many of these little Norfolk heaths, overgrown with green and silver shrubs): the place-names reinforce the notion of typical Englishness. A lovely lane, and quite deserted.

In Castle Acre I found myself back among people, drawn there perhaps by the castle and the priory (there is a good view of the priory from the far bank of the river as you ride on), or perhaps by the several pubs. The Ostrich – I chose it because it looked quiet from the outside: inside, it was packed, but pleasant – displayed above the bar a bewildering multitude of certificates and awards for culinary excellence and alcoholic expertise. My order, half a bitter and a cheese sandwich, did not much test either cellar or kitchen, but both were excellent, and very welcome.

Pleasant valley scenery continues for another half dozen miles beyond Castle Acre. At Narford Hall you catch a glimpse, behind the odd but impressive Hall itself, of the large ornamental lake which adorns its grounds.

Past Narborough, you have to contend with the proximity of the very busy A47 trunk road. To avoid it as far as possible, I took a dog-leg route on lanes across the rather scruffy levels. I rode alongside a sizeable water-filled gravel-pit, not shown on my OS map (1987 printing) even though it was large enough for someone to have thought it worthwhile mooring a motorboat there. This particular site, I discovered, was still being worked, unlike most of the pits I had passed earlier, both on the Wensum and on the Nar, many of which are now used as fisheries. Beyond Blackborough End, a waste tip occupies another old gravel pit. I did not pass the tip, but it was signposted off my lane, the verges of which were littered with paper, cardboard, strips of filthy carpet. . . . This, I reasoned, was why the owner of Narford Hall had erected a placard on his land exhorting passers by to 'Speak up for Norfolk: Granary of England or GLC rubbish tip?' The GLC has gone, but not the rubbish. And that rubbish, until we learn to produce much less of it, has to be got rid of somewhere. Canny investors, I am told, are buying shares in big holes in the ground all over Britain.

Other and more congenial images also stay in mind from this last stretch of riding. Back near Narborough, a water-pipe led up from the filled gravel-tip, with a tractor operating a portable pump, and a little further on the revolving spray was watering a crop of maize, the misty jets glistening against the sun. These were the last dry days of a long, dry summer, and beyond Setchey, where I followed the Nar across the flatlands, the drainage ditches were also doing duty as irrigation channels. Between the embanked Nar and the cut running to the Great Ouse above King's Lynn, you are back in fen country, with black earth exposed by the autumn ploughing and varied only by rows of orchard trees in sheltered corners.

And so to Magdalen Road station. If you can arrange to end your tour at some little half-forgotten halt like this, you can keep hold until the last moment of the peace and quiet of the countryside. I strolled up and down the platform until the two-coach train came swaying into view along the track, which ran as straight as a compass needle due north and south across the levels.

5. Suffolk

My riding for this book began in Norfolk in September
1989. Then came autumn and spring rides in Kent and
Sussex, where I was returning to familiar landscapes and
extending my knowledge of them. When I went back to
East Anglia, taking the train to Sudbury in Suffolk the
following June, I was looking forward to exploring
unknown territory, for this was a region I had hardly
visited. With a sense of the likely similarities and contrasts
with Norfolk, memories of a weekend near Walberswick
three or four years before, and what I could glean from the
OS maps and from Norman Scarfe's very useful volume
The Suffolk Landscape in the series edited by W G Hoskins,
I had something to go on, but not a great deal. Geoff
Aldred, my companion on this trip as well as on my visit
to Romney Marsh (Route 5), had driven to and from
Aldeburgh, but apart from that knew Suffolk no better
than I.

So: what would we find, and how should we plan our
route?

The broad outline of the county was clear. Much of
Suffolk is a chalk plateau, not high, but quite exposed,
overlain with clay soils and farmed for grain and peas.
This was heavily wooded once, and indeed 'the woodlands'
was a common term for central Suffolk until into the
nineteenth century, but now trees remain only in small
and scattered patches. The plateau is broken here and

there by streams, and in many of the valleys there are minor roads or lanes.

West of the clay, towards Thetford and Newmarket, there is lighter, sandy soil. But the Thetford area has extensive, regimented conifer forests which often coincide with military Danger Areas: not an enticing prospect. However, there are sandy soils in the east of the county also, between the clay and the North Sea. It is evident from the map that this is one of the least developed and most inviting coastal regions in England. There are woods and heaths, small villages and compact towns, few main roads and some quiet lanes and bridle paths right by the shore.

The church of the Holy Trinity at Blythburgh, famous as the Cathedral of the Marshes, was the one building we were determined to visit. It proved memorable, and is set in lovely surroundings (see Route 4). Blythburgh apart, Suffolk is known for its wealth of fine parish churches, often enlarged and beautified in the days of the prosperous cloth and wool trade. Many of them have towers ('spires' or 'steeples' is the local term, as we saw in an inscription at Grundisburgh: see Route 3). When these were built, the masons sometimes had instructions to match or outdo some neighbouring parish's recent effort: apart from the religious meaning, the towers may signify the same kind of worldly pride that erected the fantastic spires of San Gimignano in Tuscany. These flint churches would add interest to our journey and give us a sense of Suffolk's history. We would find some good examples, no doubt, without going out of our way – and so we did, at Kersey and Grundisburgh and Lavenham.

One last aspect of the Suffolk landscape, the paucity of major roads, made our route-planning easy and pleasant. In Kent and Sussex, with their dense population and nearness to London, finding itineraries which are not impossibly circuitous yet which avoid A and (as far as possible) B roads is a difficult exercise: large areas are effectively ruled out, whatever attractions they may encompass, by this difficulty.

East Anglia presents no such problems. Suffolk's only really large town is Ipswich, and we would keep north of Ipswich. A few busy roads – perhaps half a dozen – fan out from there and from Bury St Edmunds, but these are easily avoided: it took just a moment, for instance, to cross the A45 at Blakenham going east (Route 3), and between Stowupland and Stowmarket, riding back west (Route 4), a minor road carries you above its four lanes. Most of the time you can forget about cars, for there is a very extensive lane network, well surfaced and, as you would expect in this part of England, with very few noticeable gradients.

In short, we had only to decide what kind of country we wanted to cross, and which places we wanted to visit, and we would be able to plan a quiet route to meet our wishes.

We rode 'out and back', east and then west, starting from Sudbury. This was a five-day ride, some 150 miles in all. Here it is split into two routes, one two- and one three-day trip, using Wickham Market station as their terminus and starting point respectively.

Both ways, we spent a fair part of the ride on the clay lands. East out of Sudbury, we rode across the more broken southern fringe, where streams and small rivers drain towards the Stour. This is undramatic but very pleasant country. The copses give it a wooded and varied feel, even though they are mostly quite small, and the relief is broken enough to bring further variety – shifting

views and perspectives, and those constant small changes
in gradient and occasional steeper slopes which mean so
much on a bicycle.

Riding back west across the dome of the plateau, the
country was more open, with fewer trees and longer flat
stretches. Either side of Debenham there were times when
the plain had a bleak air to it, even though it was June
and the sun was generally shining. Certainly this prairie-
like landscape would pall if you had too much of it, and
you need to find some variation. This we did by taking a
green lane to get right among the crops (see the text for
Route 4). And where we could, we followed stream valleys:
here, as in Norfolk, streams which dissect the plain create
an atmosphere of their own. Norman Scarfe rightly insists
that picking out these water-courses and understanding
how they modify the terrain 'is a most delightful part of
the process of getting to know the landscape: as essential
to the discriminating tourist as to the working farmer'.

Route 3 ends in wonderfully quiet coastal scenery. The
coast is further explored in the first part of Route 4:
Aldeburgh, Thorpeness, and the heaths near Dunwich.
These heaths are a carefully conserved lowland wilderness,
on a small scale, but large enough to allow some
distinctive walks (we took to bridle paths and pushed our
bikes).

Did we choose the right route, the elusive ideal ride which
would show us as many faces of Suffolk as possible in the
time we had, while avoiding busy roads and dull country?
Certainly we saw the essential contrast between the clay
and the sand, and within each region we had variety –
metalled lanes and green lanes, heaths and woods, open
plains and hidden valleys. Main roads, as I have said, we
easily avoided. Our way back west threatened to grow

uneventful once or twice, but 'dull country' would be a harsh term for those few miles.

One obvious alternative does, however, suggest itself. If you can spare a day or two more than we had, you might ride from Blythburgh (Route 4) north by way of the Elmhams (grid reference 310840) to the valley of the Waveney. Then you could follow the river upstream, south and west. Would this be better? Would the main roads which sometimes follow the river's north-west bank spoil the ride, with traffic noise and fumes heard and smelt on the little lanes across the water where you would ride? Might those lanes themselves turn out to be a little busy? Would the attractions of the route, obvious on the map, outweigh all such problems anyway? Until I ride there, I cannot tell. You can find out for yourself – as, one day, I intend to do.

Accommodation on the more inland stretches of these roads needs advance research: you should get a bed and breakfast guide, because the villages on your way are mostly quite small and sometimes some way apart. Once you look up suitable establishments in a guidebook, you will find there is a reasonable choice, however. Geoff and I camped out. If you opt to do the same, you will need to ask farmers (or find quiet places beside green lanes), for there are few official sites. The coast, and especially Aldeburgh, offers a range of accommodation, and here you should be able to pick and choose, though in the high season booking ahead will be advisable.

We picked Sudbury station as our starting point because it lies in a smallish town, is reached with only one simple change (at Marks Tey on the Harwich line from Liverpool Street), and is currently the only Suffolk station included in Network SouthEast, which can save money for card-holders. Other lines run north from Ipswich via Stowmarket to Norwich and to Bury St Edmunds and beyond; and also, most usefully, up the coast to Lowestoft. Wickham Market, the halfway point at which the two routes given here are divided, is on this latter line.

Route 3:

South Suffolk – Sudbury, Kersey, Iken Marshes

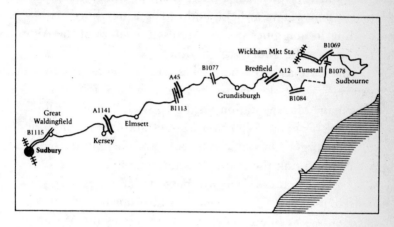

Sudbury to Wickham Market

Getting off the two-coach branch line diesel train at Sudbury station, we told the guard we were planning to ride to the coast.

'That's a long way,' was his response. 'You'd have done better to take the Lowestoft line.'

Here, evidently, was a man unfamiliar with the notion that cycling might be a pleasure in itself. This lovely trip might have enlightened him. The sea always makes an attractive goal, and when we arrived we found (as I had found in North Norfolk) quiet coastlands and unhurried towns. Riding east, you will register the changes in the landscape: from the subtly modulated relief of the clay country, through the narrow pastoral valley of the Deben (where you may spot that rare creature, an East Anglian cow), into the forests and sandy fields and patches of surviving heath south-west of Snape. There are pretty villages too: Kersey, Grundisburgh, Ufford.

Here and there, we left the quiet lanes to take bridle paths: a grassy 'green road' a little before Grundisburgh, a long and very pleasant stretch of sandy-shingly forest track below Bentwaters airfield, and finally a tree-lined path leading to magnificent views across the curve of the Alde to the peaceful Aldeburgh skyline.

The route as given here takes you out on a brief tour of sandy, sea-girt Iken Marshes and then back inland to Wickham Market station on the Ipswich–Lowestoft line. Route 4 begins at Wickham Market and takes you straight to Aldeburgh. Of course it is easy, and delightful, to do as we did and link the two routes into one four- or five-day ride – in which case you will not ride back west to Wickham Market from Iken, but turn northwards and pick up Route 4 at Snape where the road passes the Maltings concert hall and crosses the Alde river at the head of its beautiful estuary.

Sudbury to Wickham Market

Distance: approx. 64 miles. OS 155, 156

Duration: Two days (one or two overnight stops)

Terrain: Very easy. The route follows bridle paths in two places, but alternatives on lanes and B roads are readily apparent on the OS maps.

Itinerary: Trains run to **Sudbury** from London Liverpool Street (change at Marks Tey).

Leave Sudbury on the B1115 for Great Waldingfield, where you fork right on lanes at grid ref. 903433. Follow lanes just N of E via Lynn Hall and Rose Green to **Kersey** (grid ref. 000442) (10 miles).

Ride E from Kersey to join the A1141, which you take N for less than 1 mile, forking right on lanes at grid ref. 010452. Ride via Whatfield (grid ref. 025465), E to Elmsett, then NE to Offton Place (grid ref. 075490). Take lane E via Somersham and Little Blakenham to join the B1113, turning left and riding N to fork right at grid ref. 122499 and pass beneath the A45 trunk road, and so (crossing onto OS sheet 156) to **Claydon** (21 miles).

From Claydon ride on lanes ENE to Henley (grid ref. 157513), crossing straight over at the crossroads and continuing NE until you take the bridle path right at Hill Farm. Rejoin metalled road (the B1077) by Berghersh House Farm, turning right and then soon left on lane for Swilland. Now take lanes zig-zagging WSW to **Grundisburgh** (grid ref. 225510) (29 miles).

Take the lane just below Burgh to Hasketon (grid ref. 250505), where you turn left and ride NE to Bredfield (grid ref. 270530), and then E via Ufford to cross the River Deben and the railway line (at grid ref. 304519). Continue SSE across the A1152 to reach the B1084 (at grid ref. 314504). Turn right and take next lane left, riding N for 1 mile before turning right on the forest track (public bridleway) by the hamlet of Friday Street (39 miles).

Follow this track E for a little over 2 miles and then at Wantisden Corner (grid ref. 367515) head just E of N to reach the B1078 less than 1 mile E of Tunstall. From here there is a variety of possible routes exploring the woods and heaths by Iken. One suggestion is as follows. Ride N to join the B1069 at grid ref. 371558. Ride NE for a few hundred yards, taking the first lane right, and then riding a circular route starting at Ikencliffe House (grid ref. 395561), via Iken and Sudbourne (grid ref. 412530) and back to Ikencliffe House (54 miles). From here ride W back to the B1069, and so via Tunstall and right on the B1078 to **Wickham Market station** (grid ref. 326558) (64 miles).

Trains run from Wickham Market via Ipswich to London Liverpool Street.

Not far out of Sudbury, Geoff and I stopped for lunch in a field. They were cutting grass for silage. In that respect, the place was uncharacteristic of the Suffolk we saw, which was almost exclusively arable farming where it was not heath and forest. But in other ways the view contained much that was to prove typical. The gentle dip and rise of the land, with pale green fields patched with darker copses; the line of trees closing the horizon; the two flint church towers (one of them, probably, the massive tower of St Peter and St Paul, Lavenham); the melancholy pallor of dead elms in the hedgerows – all these elements were repeated again and again as we rode east.

It is difficult to pinpoint which subtle alterations account for the increased charm that the scenery can suddenly acquire in this undramatic farming country. A slightly more broken relief, narrower lanes, deeper woods, vivid colours where flax grows or poppies bloom thickly in some unsprayed corner? It is hard to know, but you respond at once. Approaching Kersey this first afternoon, and again the next morning dropping on snaky lanes out of Grundisburgh to Hasketon, we both felt a sudden lifting of the spirit as an ordinary pastoral prettiness gave way to something more remarkable.

Our visit to Kersey was a lucky chance. We had not picked it out, and did not realise it was a celebrated beauty spot. I have the postcard in front of me as I write, stuck up on the wall above my desk.

The single lane has timber-framed houses, some of them washed in the well-known Suffolk pink. Terraces of old brick are weathered to a glowing red, and other buildings have decorative plaster work (pargetting), also an East Anglian speciality. At the bottom of the village is a ford or watersplash – a moorhen, untroubled by passing humans, wandered upstream as we crossed – and then the lane rises to St Mary's church.

Clothmaking was once the source of Kersey's wealth, as is the case in many Suffolk and Norfolk villages and towns. Then, with the shifting of the wool trade to Yorkshire during the seventeenth century, the village became a small farming settlement, something of a backwater. A rural backwater used to mean having no mains water or electricity, at least until the 1950s. Now, of course, in such a place as Kersey (dubbed by Pevsner 'the most picturesque village of South Suffolk'), it means a commuter settlement, a place people retire to, a mecca for tourists. Two pubs, a restaurant, a potter's workshop, notices beseeching coach and car drivers to park considerately . . . even so, tourism was less obtrusive here than we found it later at Lavenham (Route 4), and tourists themselves were thin on the ground this Thursday.

The church, built mostly between the twelfth and the fifteenth centuries, has good views down through the village and over the surrounding country, prettily broken where the River Brett and a tributary stream cut through the clay plateau. In the building's fabric, Geoff drew my attention to the use of knapped and squared flints, whose dark blue lustre contrasts pleasantly with the whitish-brown of the unworked flint rubble used for less decorative, extensive surfaces, for example in the walls of the tower. Another characteristic feature of Suffolk churches to be seen here in Kersey is the flushwork panelling (stone inlaid decoratively with the flint) of the tower battlements and the south porch.

Time to push on, though it was becoming apparent that our original aim of reaching the forested heathlands by evening had been quite unrealistic.

Across through Whatfield and Elmsett and Offton Place (a decorative gable-end in Dutch style). Then came Somersham, with a rural Village Stores, the kind of shop you no longer find in most of East Sussex or Kent. In the yard of a grain wholesaler three gleaming new trucks were

parked beneath clean-lined vertical silos and horizontal
barns. I love the shapes of agricultural-industrial buildings,
though their materials – corrugated iron, concrete, asbestos
– are hardly rural these days. Also, I enjoy seeing links in
the chain between field and dinner-plate – as we did the
next day, on Iken Marshes, where we had to climb the
bank to squeeze past giant pea-harvesting machines in tiny
lanes.

Daydreaming about grainstores by railroads in vast
Canadian prairies, and the branch line into the sugar
works at Mallow in County Cork, I floated out of
Somersham and through the inevitable blur of nondescript
semi-industry along the busy A45: tall chimney of a kiln,
glistening ponds in worked-out pits, the hum of speeding
tyres.

We put up our tents by a green lane. 'Campsite,' my notes
say. 'Hares, larks. Hedgerows. Dead elms. *Cold at night.*'
And then: 'Leaving next a.m., oak-framed tiled barn,
decrepit, savable. Lodge at lane end: beautifully tended
garden, hedged all around. Pleasantly informal glass
porch/conservatory: cat, grandfather clock.'

Travelling on a bike, passing plenty of houses slowly
enough to form some images of them and their ways, you
find yourself inventing other lives. . . . It would be nice to
be one of these Suffolk gardeners, for instance, who keep
their vegetable plots so splendidly. Back home, for all the
work Kate and I were putting in, our peas and beans were
backward, the weeds were rampant: but here – perhaps
the lightness of the sandy soils, lighter and sandier as we
rode east, makes the work less taxing? – perfect results
mocked from behind every hedge and fence: weedless and
dead-straight lines of thriving spuds in flower, four-foot-
high beanrows weighed down with bulging pods. . . . Or it

might be nice (for half an hour) to be that cat who sprawls on the table under the glass roof, opening one eye as two laden cyclists push past, then yawning, dozing again in the steady beat of the old clock. . . . But then again it might be more fun to be one of those cyclists, moving on, swinging through the lanes to Grundisburgh (and remarking how those lanes, with their sudden right angles, trace centuries-old field boundaries: unlike the straight lanes of High Norfolk where parliamentary enclosure had such an impact).

Grundisburgh's church and shops and post office are grouped attractively around the green, where a stream flows under a bridge and you can sit on a bench and see the world go not too quickly by. A mother duck and ten ducklings paddled obligingly downstream as we watched.

The church's tower, like several others in Suffolk, was enlarged at the expense of a local magnate. You usually have to consult guidebooks to discover who paid for the work, but here at Grundisburgh a plaque on the tower ('steeple' is the local term, and need not imply a spire) tells all:

> This Steeple Was Built
> The Bells Set in Order
> And Fixt At The Charge
> Of ROBERT THINGE Gent
>   Lately Deceased AD 1731–1732

Beyond the Deben valley, crossed at Ufford with its Dutch-looking gables, comes a striking change in the soil and the vegetation. Just by our bridge over the river a pump was driving water up the slope to a great revolving spray on the ridge above: sand, potatoes. Then we rode through felled and half-cleared conifers, with currant bushes grown in the clearings. At Friday Street, wheeling

our bikes past forestry workers' houses, we explored a
large plantation: lunch in the warm sun, followed by a lazy
stroll along the edge of the wood where it borders the
airfield. This is a pleasantly loose, open wood, unlike the
dense and regimented forestry on the Breckland by
Thetford. Birches and oaks grow along the margins and
the big pines themselves are mature and well spaced.

Towards the end of the walk – the dry but shifting
surface would have made riding hard work – the country
opened up to give park-like views away to the south. And
indeed this is a park, Staverton Park and the Thicks,
celebrated among botanists and ecologists because it is
very probably a specimen of primeval oak-forest, enclosed
direct from the original woods in the thirteenth century or
even earlier.

A much more modern sight, one that nobody could have
seen in Suffolk until the last four decades, met our eyes on
the other side of the track. Here, a newly ploughed and
harrowed field stretched into the trees, acres of the purest
golden sand like a child's enormous dream. How this soil
must blow off, by the ton, when the fields are bare and the
wind gets up. Good crops require constant irrigation in a
dry year: it was as recently as 1947 that the technique was
used (for the first time in Britain) here in the Sandlings.
Down by a pool in the Butley river to our right a diesel
pump was hammering on, and a network of metal pipes
distributed the water to nozzles that sprayed it out over
the potato-plants just coming into purple flower.

And Bentwaters airfield, whose perimeter fence our track
had followed among the trees? This is a USAF nuclear
base. It was spoken of in early 1990 as a possible site for
the new air-launched cruise missiles which Britain was
agreeing to host as our contribution to celebrating the end
of the Cold War. In the woods, the base is hardly

obtrusive . . . but as we came out and returned to metalled lanes, we took a wrong turning and ended up at the main gate. No, said the young pistol-toting guard, there was no way through. He seemed pretty laid back – but barked out sharp enough when the front wheel of Geoff's bike strayed onto the pink line painted across the road. Geoff drew back, and the guard said (predictably) that while *he* cared nothing for these rules, 'some of those guys inside . . .' (he jerked his thumb over his shoulder).

We rode away, back downhill. The airfield can be ignored, and before long you get right away from it. However, military airfields have a place in my mental map of East Anglia. An awareness of their presence – Bentwaters, Woodbridge, Swaffham – modifies my sense of this part of England. (And there is Sizewell nuclear power station, too, whose double row of high pylons, striding towards Ipswich, switched back and forth above our route.)

Iken Marshes lie below the great curve which the River Alde makes when, having all but reached the sea below Aldeburgh, it swings back behind the shingle bank and runs parallel to the shore for half a dozen miles. That shingle bank, Orford Ness, is a bleak, salty place, inaccessible by road. Iken Marshes are more hospitable, and delightfully quiet too: light sands, with conifer forest and patches of heath and, between the woods and the shore, a belt of farmland where they were growing potatoes, strawberries and peas.

Not only growing, but harvesting. This looks an exposed place but it evidently has a very 'early' climate: frost-free most years, perhaps, because of the closeness of the wide estuary? Coming out of Snape, we saw trailers being loaded with spuds, and then by Iken village we were held up by a convoy of three massive pea-harvesting machines approaching us down the tiny lane. We mounted the bank and squeezed past: each machine breathed over us a strong, almost heady, waft of pea-pod and crushed pea-stalk. They cost (we were told later) as much as £100,000 apiece. Farmers work under contract to Birds Eye, whose freezing plant is at Lowestoft. Birds Eye own the harvesters, which strip pods from plants and peas from pods, and they own the trucks which leave the harvest-field for the factory every twenty minutes: they are not allowed to stand waiting longer and must drive off after that time whether they have a full load or not.

Following a bridle path between hedgerow trees out towards the curve of the river, we came out at the top of a field with views across water and moored yachts to Aldeburgh. The farmer was there, standing beside his four-wheel drive car, chatting over the fence to his neighbour. Could we put up our tents? Would it be all right if we lit a fire? He was friendly and welcoming.

So we made camp, and enjoyed the warm late afternoon. Few arrivals at the seaside could have been more idyllic. What an attractive coast this is. What a delight it is to turn away from the water and look inland over fields and small farms and woodland, instead of over tarmac and traffic signs and villas.

Iken Marshes, near Aldeburgh, 7.30pm, 15 June 1990

Across the wide sweep of the Alde estuary, the rooves of Aldeburgh: red tiles, and also the black slate roof and white-framed mansard windows of one particularly imposing building. A Dutch look.

Between us and the river, a sloping sandy field, planted with what I suppose is a 'green manure': a vetch-like plant. We have seen a small rabbit, a child's ideal bunny, scurrying between the rows – and also a thin, alert, black-eared hare, which came through a hedge-gap from the next field, stood poised, turned its head from side to side, then caught sight of us (or smelled us) and ran back.

In the river, the yachts, prows to the ebb tide, stand moored to orange buoys.

Beyond the river, before Aldeburgh, is a broad strip of water-meadow. There is a large herd of black-and-white cows, strung in a clustering line in the evening sun. (After our two grey, warmish days, cooler at evening, the sun has broken strongly through the clearing sky in the last couple of hours, and it is now hotter than it has been since we left Sudbury.)

A cuckoo calls from a thicket somewhere below the town. All around, birds are singing – apart from that, it is almost silent.

Route 4:

The Sandlings, the Blyth Valley and the Suffolk Plateau

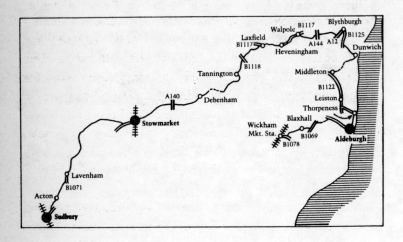

Wickham Market to Sudbury

Once you are riding west over the clay plateau, this route is easy, spacious going . . . though perhaps (some may find) a little lacking in variety. Turning to me as we rolled between peas and barley – was this before Tannington, on Sunday, or before Stowmarket on Monday? – Geoff said: 'This is what it's like driving across the American Midwest.'

The feel of the land must change markedly with the seasons. Everything was green, in June, when we were there. Later must come a beautiful contrast, in fine harvest weather, between golden grainfields, brown earth where the peas have been harvested, and still-green hedges. Then winter, with endless bare land and bare-branched trees open to the sea wind, cowering and sprawling under a rainy sky. Perhaps only an eccentric such as myself could find any pleasure in cycling there then – and even I would want the wind behind me.

Two strategies made our ride back west more various. Above Blythburgh and again after Stowmarket, we followed river valleys, which dissect the plain and interlace its airy spaces with more tangled and secluded landscapes: poplar plantations, cows in weedy pastures, lanes switching across green trickles on narrow bridges. The Blyth does not amount to much once you move inland from its spreading estuary, and the tributary of the Gipping which took us from Stowmarket to Rattlesden lacks even a name, but small though they are these streams make a world of their own.

Another element of variety came from taking a stretch of paths and tracks a little before Debenham. Looking closely at the OS map, you will see that there are similar opportunities just after that attractive little town; or further back, by Saxtead (grid reference 248658); or, a little south of the way we went, near Pettaugh on the A1120 Stowmarket road. Old drovers' roads, which I take many of these clearly marked but sometimes quite neglected routes to be, may be rideable in places (at any rate with a mountain bike), but in other places they may be hopelessly bumpy or wildly overgrown: the last stretch of bridleway we took made me want to add a new category, 'temperate-zone jungle', to the accepted topographical divisions of Suffolk.

It is the clay plateau that I have been writing about, and most of this ride is on the clay. It begins, however, in altogether different country – the sandy, heathy coastal strip where Route 3 left off. Aldeburgh, and in its different style Thorpeness, are rewarding towns. Then your way is over the heaths, to Blythburgh, where there is a magnificent parish church not to be missed by anyone visiting the Suffolk coast.

Wickham Market to Sudbury

Distance: approx. 90 miles. OS 156, 155

Duration: Three days (two overnight stops)

Terrain: Very easy. One stretch of bridle path proved very tangled, but an alternative on lanes is readily apparent on the OS map.

Itinerary: Trains run to **Wickham Market** via Ipswich.

Leave Wickham Market on the B1078, riding ENE for about 1 mile and then turning off left (at grid ref. 339560) to follow lanes via Blaxhall to the crossing of the Alde at The Maltings. Past the Inn at Snape Street, take the lane right, and when this lane swings N (at grid ref. 401584) continue down the track, left of the farm cottages, and so NE to the A1094, which you take right to **Aldeburgh** (10 miles).

Take the coastal lane N from Aldeburgh to Thorpeness. Then comes a stretch of B roads: the B1353 and then right on the B1122 to Leiston, and N from Leiston on the B1122 via Theberton, shortly after which you fork right on the B1125. Cross the Minsmere river and then after another hundred yards or so follow the bridle path NE over the heath. Cross straight over the first lane you come to (at grid ref. 445685) and then take the next lane left to the crossroads at grid ref. 450693. From here you can proceed via a track and the B1125 direct to Blythburgh. However, to see the heaths, and Dunwich, you will do better to follow our route: right on the lane to Dunwich, then back NW on the lane to rejoin the B1125 at grid ref. 450726. From here ride N to **Blythburgh** (27 miles).

Leave Blythburgh SW on the A12, taking the first lane right (at grid ref. 449749). Pass Wenhaston Hall, cross the river, and turn left at grid ref. 428749 to ride WSW, crossing the A144. Follow the lane under the railway and sharp left. Then turn right at the T-junction (grid ref. 393738) and so to Walpole. Follow the B1117 SW to Heveningham, and then continue to follow the river on lanes via Ubbeston church (grid ref. 323726) until this lane climbs away from the valley, and you follow it round to **Laxfield** (grid ref. 293723) (40 miles).

Ride just S of W from Laxfield, crossing the B1116 at Wells Corner and then turning left off the lane at grid ref. 269719. Turn right after less than 1 mile, heading SW to the B1118 at Crown Corner. Cross the B road at this staggered junction and continue on the lane, SSW via Tannington to the lane junction by Saxtead Little Green (grid ref. 248658). Here turn right and follow this lane round to the T-junction at grid ref. 217642. At this point you can take lanes via Kenton, making two sides of a triangle, or a rather more direct route via tracks (which are, however, bumpy in places and very overgrown in others: impassable in wet weather), to **Debenham** (grid ref. 175635) (53 miles).

Riding SW and then W, via Mickfield (grid ref. 135618) (crossing here onto OS sheet 155), you come to the A140. Cross this via the staggered junction and continue W via Middlewood Green to Saxham Street (grid ref. 087615). Staying on lanes via Walnut Tree Farm and Thorney Green, join the B1115 and so into **Stowmarket** (62 miles).

Ride W, first on the B1115 and then on lanes, to Rattlesden (grid ref. 980590). Stay with the stream past White House Farm to the marked spot height, 62m, at grid ref. 957579. Here turn left and ride on lanes almost due S to Brettenham (grid ref. 956535), SSW to Preston St Mary (grid ref. 943503), and so to **Lavenham** (grid ref. 917495) (77 miles).

From Lavenham, leaving S on the B1071 but turning off right at grid ref. 913485, follow lanes via Acton (grid ref. 895447) to **Sudbury** (90 miles).

Trains run from Sudbury to London Liverpool Street, via Marks Tey.

On the south wall of the Moot Hall in Aldeburgh, an Elizabethan building elaborately restored in the nineteenth century, is a sundial with the inscription *Horas non numero nisi serenas*: 'I only count the peaceful hours'. An apt epigraph for this trip as a whole. Just north of Aldeburgh, however, you may find peace quite elusive. The B roads were not dangerously busy (on a fine midsummer Saturday), but once you have become accustomed to the silence and sweet air of lanes and byways, even a minor classified road is a noisy smelly place.

To reach Aldeburgh, we had taken a grassgrown track north-east from the river crossing at Snape. It became a lane of slithering, shifting sand, between hedgerow trees and asparagus fields. Then three miles of main road: golfcourse, clubhouse, solid bourgeois suburbs.

Then suddenly you are in the old town, with its wide main street parallel to the beach. Alleys and open courts give you glimpses of the sea as you wander from shop to shop (we were buying a picnic). The bank of shingle drops sharply to the water. Geoff talked vaguely about swimming: perhaps now, perhaps later. . . . Easterly breezes and bright sunshine had tanned our faces and sapped our (easily sapped) moral and athletic purposiveness. Was there, really, any need to hurry? Sun-warmed air flowed up from the blue sea over the hot stones, so that the view north to Thorpeness was seen through shimmering waves like flaws in thick glass. Far out, its movement made leisurely by the distance, shipping made way south for Harwich and Felixstowe or north for Scandinavia. A family crunched past, dressed for the beach, the little girl stooping to pick up a handful of small stones.

Geoff finished his coffee, scooped out a more comfortable resting-place in the shingle, stretched in the yellow light, closed his eyes: zzz . . . *horas non numero nisi serenas*. . . .

The position of the Moot Hall, which must once have been central but which now lies just back from the beach and the fish-houses, shows how erosion has eaten away this coast and drowned its ports. At Dunwich, seven or eight miles north, nothing but a hamlet remains of what was once a thriving town. Aldeburgh is thriving still, at once elegant and four-square, leisured and maritime. Each tarred fish-house along the front has its winch, its slipway, its nets hung out to dry. Small-scale, picturesque fishing.

Thorpeness, two miles north of Aldeburgh, is a planned holiday settlement built over a 25-year period from 1911 under the careful scrutiny of the landlord, Glencairn Stuart Ogilvie. The original plans were modified, then abandoned, and nowadays people live here all year round, but some trace of Ogilvie's conception persists, and gives Thorpeness a special character. According to the brochure you can buy in the gift shop – itself a singular document, with its archaic tone of deference to 'the Estate' – Ogilvie's aim was 'to build a fantasy holiday village which held no attraction for the "day trippers"'. It was to be a place where well-to-do families rented salubrious accommodation at high rates. An artificial lake studded with artificial islands named after scenes and characters from J M Barrie; a transplanted windmill; the 'House in the Clouds', a steel-framed water tower whose upper part is disguised as a weather-boarded Suffolk cottage – these are the elements of fantasia, quaint and inoffensive by the standards of today's theme parks. For the rest, the settlement consists of housing in a jumble of styles, given some homogeneity by the general use of timber treated with pitch as a facing for the concrete blocks, mass-produced on site, of which most of the buildings are made.

The result is not unattractive, certainly less unattractive than such settlements as Peacehaven, thrown up at roughly the same period without any overall plan.

However, the utopian-paternal hand of Mr Ogilvie perhaps
feels a little heavy. His notion of fantasy was a little
mawkish, perhaps. Peeping in through an open door at the
interior of the abandoned Country Club, we thought what
a good place it would be for a three-day-long party. Its
steel roofgirders and concrete floor made a dimly
cavernous space. You'd wander out at three in the
morning and slither down sandhills to the beach.

So to Leiston. Would this be a boom town, the pubs filled
with high-spending construction workers from nearby
Sizewell? I recalled the frenzied and sinister atmosphere I
had detected, or imagined, cycling a few years ago through
the rather bleak, rather anonymous little settlements on
the Cap de la Hague, centre of the French nuclear
reprocessing industry ('*Cotentin, poubelle atomique*' was the
slogan painted on walls in Cherbourg). Leiston's pubs
looked busy, but so far as I could judge from my bike, the
drinking was boisterous rather than frenetic.

After crossing the Minsmere river at Middleton, you
find yourself among the heaths of the Sandlings. Inland
from Dunwich there is an extensive nature reserve, to
which access is restricted. Some of the adjacent heaths,
however, are common land, where you can wander freely.
It is well worth taking your bike (as we did) along bridle
paths in among the bracken, the heather, the pale sand
and the slim white birches: a landscape whose colours you
would associate with bog or mountain, rather than with
lowland England. It is worthwhile, too, allowing time to
wander in the lanes which run between the main road and
the coast at Walberswick, Dunwich and Dunwich common:
heaths, woods, low cliffs and shingle beaches, the sea.

The heaths that run north from Aldeburgh are broken
by the broad, shallow curve of the Blyth estuary.

Something of the beauty of Blythburgh's famous church ('the Cathedral of the Marshes' – it is dedicated to the Holy Trinity) derives from its setting above the water-meadows just at the estuary's head. But its architecture would be memorable anywhere. Like many East Anglian churches, it is at one level a memorial to the former secular prosperity of the town. Most of it dates from the earlier fifteenth century. Before 1500, a decline set in: ships were growing too large for that shallow harbour, trade deserted Blythburgh ('the Bretons did not come this year with salt': 1478), and the town lost its Mint and its twice-yearly Fair. The materials of the well-restored interior, the limewashed walls and brick flooring, recreate the original decor and bring out the simple, airy and perfect proportions. Aloft in the roof are carved and painted wooden angels, faded with age, some of them pockmarked by the bullets fired at them by Cromwellian troops.

What strikes you as you look at the building from outside, and what I think chiefly accounts for its particular synthesis of gravity and grace, is how the dark flint walls – flint tends to severity, even though here it is worked with great care and decorated with paler stone parapets and flushwork – carry the great flight of clerestory windows that run like a shaft of light from end to end of the church.

Camping just south of Blythburgh on Saturday night, we visited the church before matins on Sunday. Then, crossing our last patch of heath, climbing north and west by Bramfield, we approached the boundary between the sand and the clay.

A placard advertised asparagus for sale. We turned down the farm track to find a fine solid brick house fronted by a sweep of lawn. At the back, a wooden table was set out with new carrots, turnips, broad beans, raspberries, strawberries – the asparagus was just finished. We ate the first few delicious strawberries from the punnet we had bought and chatted to the family, two generations, or perhaps three, for the old man who stood sunning himself seemed as likely to be the grandfather as the father of the talkative farmer. This was a thriving, well-tended market garden, pleasantly uncommercial in atmosphere, but obviously doing good business: passing trade like ourselves, but mainly fruit and vegetables for freezing in Lowestoft. We were told about the differing qualities of the sand and the clay. Small farmers could make money on this sand only if they irrigated. Here, they had a million-gallon yearly licence from the (French-owned) Anglian Water Authority. The water was metered and every gallon had to be paid for, even though the well was on the farmer's own land.

At the corner of the lane, we stopped and dispatched the rest of the strawberries. The broad beans and carrots we would eat with butter as an hors-d'oeuvre that night . . . they were excellent.

The dwindling Blyth took us up through Walpole, past landscaped Heveningham Hall, past Ubbeston where the brick-towered church has been converted to an attractive private house. Climbing out of the valley, pausing on the bank by the lane, we enjoyed the sudden opening out which came as we left the tangled streamside with its hedges and shadows: small contrasts, in this undemonstrative landscape, but appreciated to the full.

At Laxfield, Geoff greatly admired the old pub with its oak settles and beer in barrels, tucked away by the church, where he bought a couple of pints of Adnam's ale poured into a lemonade bottle for drinking later.

We found a fine spot for our last night's camp, under well-spaced oaks by the side of a green lane. An early stop left us time to wander between the wide pea-fields, drink tea, sketch, write.

Near Monk Soham church, 4.30pm, 17 July 1990

The day has fallen into four stretches. Sandy heath either side of Blythburgh, river valleys with cows and greenery, a long open run through pea- and barley-fields of the plateau. Fourth and last, this just-rolling country. What pleasure, after an hour of sheer flatness, the eye takes in the return of variety, even the long mild declivities of mid-Suffolk.

Geoff is sketching next to me. Not using any horizontal lines, he says – avoiding heavy lines in the background, so as not to lose depth.

What he is sketching is a rutted dry grass track (on which, not that he is drawing them, stand a primus, a bottle of milk, a kettle, and other implements of tea-making). Beyond, a large field of young pea-plants. Birds kept off this by regular explosions from a calor-gas birdscarer (no Jude with rattle) 100 yards from where we sit.

At the fall of night, we found to our relief that some timing device or light-sensitive switch turned this noisy machine off. I suppose if you stayed long enough its sudden bangs would cease to shock you. The local rabbits seemed inured. Geoff pointed one out, standing in the peas, ears pricked as if waiting: *bang!* the creature didn't move, probably didn't even blink. Probably went on eating pea-stalks.

I made my own rough sketch of the view:

The field dips out of sight, the land rises again, more peas (?), dark green hedgerow, a field of barley. A lane runs across, from time to time a car passes. Beyond this, framed by dark trees which make the skyline, square-towered and flint-built like almost every Suffolk church we've seen, rises Monk Soham church. We are a mile or two from it. It is the natural focus for this view.

As I finished making notes, two boys came by on bikes,

local children, exploring this track for the first time. We
warned them that the path would become rough and
unrideable further on, where hardcore and buckled old
tarmac underlay the grass. Indeed, as we had seen from
public notices posted here and there, this track was to
undergo a change of legal status, from 'road used as a
public path' to 'bridleway'. In law, cyclists will still be
able to use it. But will it degenerate further, overgrow with
thickets of weeds and brambles until it becomes
impassable?

Next morning, we made our way, with some perversity,
along what we could see at the outset would be a well-nigh
impassable path. Up early, soon off, we plunged light-
heartedly down this jungle track. Brambles, tall weeds wet
with dew, reached out their tendrils to clasp our spokes
and soak our clothes. Lying between parallel rows of well-
grown trees, this must have been an old established path,
marking perhaps some field or parish boundary (though no
boundary is shown here on the modern map). The
overhanging, thick-leaved summer branches kept the week-
old rains wet in the ground. We had to clamber round
marshy puddles and skirt stretches of yellow sticky clay.

Geoff walked in front. The handlebars and front wheel
of his bike were a kind of icebreaker, cutting a narrow
passage through stems and stalks, dew and sap. Pollen
flew up in clouds, visible puffs like jets of steam in the
steamy air, warm already at six o'clock. Burrs and thorns
and big winged seeds anchored themselves in our clothes.

Daylight and champaign! We were out, on an open
track by Hill Farm.

The buildings, including a fine brick-built milking
parlour (so they did have cows here once), were decaying,
but from here on the track was evidently still in use by

machines. It was like reaching the smooth beach at the edge of a mangrove swamp. And not before time – the rich cocktail of pollens had brought on a spectacular attack of hay fever.

Sniffing and sneezing, I rode on. The symptoms, and the drugs I took to tame them, have left me with a slightly hazy memory of the next part of our journey. Like a pleasantish daydream under the influence of a slight temperature: stirring, fluid, vague.

Up on the clay plateau, just before crossing the A140, we sprawled on a bank drinking coffee, noisy tractors vibrating past in the lane, pea-fields and strips of copse all around us. Then at Stowmarket, waiting at the level crossing, I recall admiring the fine Victorian station (in Elizabethan style), and thinking, when at last the goods train rolled across, how pleasant a day the guard must be enjoying, sitting in his open van, watching Suffolk roll away.

Leafy stream valley, to Rattlesden: fixing a puncture, making more coffee in a nettle-grown shed, out of the rising wind – the sky was greying, starting to threaten rain.

Our last stop was at Lavenham, well known for its prettiness, with half-timbered halls and houses and a big church that rivals Blythburgh's in grandeur but not (we felt) in grace. However, we did scant justice to this church. The pie shop had been our first priority, and it was in the churchyard that we ate our pies, looking up at the tower. The road by the churchyard is called Potland Lane, and the gross name seemed apt. A passing villager said how pleasant it was to see tourists enjoying Lavenham's heritage, and his dog meanwhile displayed a lively interest in those few of our pies that were still uneaten.

Then on to Sudbury, getting a little lost, having another

puncture, passing a curious farmstead whose barn walls were decorated with gaudy primitive murals. We rushed down into the town, taking wrong turnings in our haste, putting each other right. Just in time for the 2.55, we were at the station, where the trip had begun five days ago.

At first, flopping into the warm seats, observing that the rain had considerately held off until we were aboard, we enjoyed stillness, recuperation. A hectic finish to the journey. Then, even before reaching Marks Tey where we would have to change to the main line for unimaginable Liverpool Street, unimaginable London, we began to recall the many pleasures of Suffolk and to discuss how and when we might come back for more.

6. Kent

Kentish readers might want to accuse me of taking a rather Sussex-based view of their county. The three routes in this chapter actually begin just over the border into Sussex, and two of them, being round trips, finish in Sussex, too. However, I have found routes which cross some quintessentially Kentish landscapes and which reflect the growing pleasure and sense of discovery with which I cycled in this county, revisiting familiar places and exploring new ones. The railway from Charing Cross and Waterloo to Tunbridge Wells and Hastings runs, I admit, just inside Sussex from Frant onwards; but it is ideally convenient, with a succession of quiet stations in rural settings all the way from Tunbridge Wells to Battle, as well as being very scenic.

You get off the train in Sussex, but within half an hour you have ridden into the Kentish Weald or into Romney Marsh. Facing north on the Weald, you have the best of Kent before you: the Weald itself, the clay vale, the line of greensand hills, and the North Downs with their often complex escarpment which gives way at the top to broad open plateaux, where corn or forests grow.

The Weald and the Marsh, the broad belt of clay (covered, in the fruit- and hop-growing district by the Teise, with kinder soil), the Downs and the strip of sandy upland which runs parallel to their escarpment and which lifts beautiful Egerton (Route 7) high above the blue plain

– these are the landscapes I explored. They amount, I
know, to an incomplete representation of the county. The
woods of the Blean above Canterbury, the Victorian
resorts of Thanet and the Channel harbours of south-east
Kent, the Medway, the Thames, much of the chalk Downs
too – these do not appear in my rides and descriptions.
Kent's nearness to London and its double seaside role as
both resort and gateway have brought urban and semi-
urban development and much heavy traffic to and through
the county. To avoid this, I drew a line roughly from
Canterbury to Tonbridge, and then north–south through
Canterbury: beyond it, I decided, to the north and east,
the density of population and the frequency of major roads
would make it depressingly difficult to find extensive quiet
rides. So I did not make the attempt, and stayed in the
south and south-west.

I am certain this was a wise decision, for even in the
more peaceful country I had chosen, each route gave me
brief but sharp reminders of Kent's role as commuter
settlement and transport corridor. However, these were
soon past, and I enjoyed much safe, quiet cycling. Kent
has little remote or wild country, but deep seclusion – the
seclusion of a glade in a tended wood or of the distant
corner of an overgrown garden – is yours if you know
where to seek it. Alongside passing moments of noise and
haste, I had hours of calm: in the hidden green lanes
between Wye, Crundale and Hassell Street (Route 5), by
the banks of the lower Teise in hop gardens near
Horsmonden and of the upper Teise at Bayham Abbey
(Route 6), and in the sheep fields by Bethersden (Route
7), with their rushy pools and lines of copse and spreading
hedgerow trees.

Much of Kent must have been quiet two centuries ago.

However, 'the population within the ancient boundaries of Kent has increased more than tenfold since 1800, and this increase is continuing' (Burnham and MacRae, *The Rural Landscape of Kent*). The effects of this great growth in population are noticeable outside the major conurbations and their suburbs. Even quiet Kentish villages and small towns often offer a visible record, legible to the least expert eye, of successive waves of building. There are Victorian villas, built for the few when commuting was a rarity and a luxury. Then come estates of the inter-war years, more modest but more extensive. Sometimes there is council housing: at Chilham, as you climb towards the aristocratic castle, you pass a fine bit of democratic popular building, a prize-winning council development on an appropriately small scale. Usually, there will be 'luxury development' of a recent date – often enough, buildings will be going up now. At Brenchley, I found two estate agents but only one grocer's shop.

More ramshackle and eccentric buildings crop up, giving a lane end or a turning in the road an incongruous shanty-town feel. On Romney Marsh, by Stelling Minnis with its common, and (more surprisingly) in picturesque Egerton, I saw 'temporary' homes, flimsy board shacks, which had evidently been in place for three or four decades.

A sympathetic interest in what has happened to Kent is better, surely, than facile rhetoric about eyesores and philistines and new barbarism. But it is idle to deny that the county suffers much, aesthetically, from unplanned sprawl, that the Medway towns are depressing, or that further unchecked development will all too quickly eat into surviving rural areas. Idle, too, to deny the impact on any walker's or cyclist's ear and eye of the major trunk routes which run from London by way of Ashford and Canterbury to the Channel ports: and here, too, the future is likely to bring more damage to Kent's delicate landscape, as cars and trains converge on the Chunnel.

Enough of this. I chose to keep away from it as far as possible: this is a book for pleasure-seeking cyclists, not a history or a lament. Those who live in Kent's busier places do at least have some lovely countryside on their doorsteps. As in East Sussex, the High Weald is the remotest and most unspoiled extensive region. Much still remains of the landscape that pleased Cobbett, not a writer to hide his adverse opinions and not a temperament much given to rhapsody. In Tenterden in 1823, he wrote:

> Here I am after a most delightful ride of twenty-four miles, through Frant, Lamberhurst, Goudhurst, Milkhouse Street, Benenden and Rolvenden. . . . The country from Frant to Lamberhurst is very woody. . . . This Lamberhurst is a very pretty place. . . . It lies in a valley with beautiful hills around it.

And he went on to note that the view from Goudhurst church covered an area 'about twenty-five miles in diameter, and the whole is over a very fine country'. Anyone following Cobbett's route now (where, though, has Milkhouse Street gone?) would notice busy traffic, and new building, but the general aspect of the countryside is still 'very woody', 'very pretty', with 'beautiful hills'. The woods have left their trace in many place-names: all those ending in 'den' and 'dene' (a typically Kentish termination, meaning 'clearing') and all those ending in 'hurst' (very common in the Sussex Weald, too: the word means 'wood').

Two of the three routes (6 and 7) are circular tours beginning and ending in the High Weald. It can be strenuous country – Route 6, in particular, involves stiff climbs up by Goudhurst and Kilndown – but it is immensely rewarding. For more about the character and

history of the High Weald, see the introduction to the East
Sussex rides (Chapter 6), two of which (Routes 9 and 10)
also explore its hills and stream valleys.

North of the Weald is a vale of clay, poor soil in itself, but
in the district south of Maidstone covered with better soil
brought down by the rivers. Here, by the Teise and its
tributaries, between Horsmonden and Marden, I had
pleasant riding (Route 6) in a patchwork of hop gardens
and orchards which justifies Kent's traditional designation
as a 'garden'. As you climb steeply to Goudhurst on the
ridge, you gaze back from winding lanes over the fields of
fruit. I went in late April, a little early for the blossom
(though in 1990, a forward year, it was beginning to
flower). Blossom-time is the time to go, and May and early
June are the months for it.

As the vale runs east, the soils are formed on the bare
clay. They are of low grade agriculturally, tough to work,
slow to drain: 'soup in winter, concrete in summer', so
they say. The landscape benefits from this intractability as
it rules out arable agribusiness. Grubbing up trees and
hedges does not pay in the poor soil. So tall, thick
hedgerows, which include handsome full-grown ash and
oak trees, enclose the small fields of permanent pasture.
From Biddenden to Pluckley (Route 7), you will enjoy
pastoral views from very quiet lanes. Everyone has at least
heard of the Weald, the orchards, the Downs, but this
corner of Kent – a dozen square miles, perhaps, around
Bethersden – I like to think of as a secret place.

Everyone has heard of Romney Marsh, too. It is
distinctive, self-contained – unique, indeed, though
Pevensey Levels in Sussex (explored in Route 10) has a
similar appearance and a similarly long history. At
Pevensey, an eighth-century charter refers to already

existing earthworks. On Romney Marsh, reclamation was begun in Roman times. Pevensey is still largely pasture, but arable farming is now widespread on the Marsh, and the famous sheep are in relative eclipse. As an extensive stretch of flat land, peaceful away from the few major roads, Romney Marsh has practical attractions for cyclists, too (though beware of heading into the wind in such unsheltered terrain).

The Marsh's quality is best brought out by contrast with some neighbouring region. In Route 5 we ride across the Marsh, then across the rather nondescript landscape to its north, and then along a stretch of the old Pilgrims' Way, into the scarp and plateau of the chalk Downs. The scarp is not high, but its complexities hide some lovely, dreaming valleys which run deep into the body of the chalk mass, as below Crundale. There are woods, too, including the big plantation of Challock Forest south-west of Chilham, where the North Downs Way bridle path offers wonderful walking (or riding, if you insist, but I got off and pushed). On the wide plateau, more woods are interspersed with cornfields. In this corner of England, jutting into the sea, you feel exposed to maritime winds and to the big sky when you emerge from the intimate, miniature landscapes of the slopes up onto these rolling spaces. Routes 5 and 7 both climb the North Downs, and Route 7 also crosses the strip of greensand hills which lies south of them and separate them from the clay vale.

Egerton, on these sand hills, epitomises (like Chilham before it) a certain Englishness which the Kentish landscape as a whole seems often to represent. I wonder if this is partly a matter of the long historical association of Canterbury with Anglican Christianity? Thomas Wyatt, the sixteenth-century courtier and poet, had this

association in mind when he wrote in his verse-letter to
John Poynz:

> But here I am in Kent and Christendom
> Among the muses where I read and rhyme.

Chaucer, too, is naturally in one's mind when
Canterbury Cathedral appears in the skyline. Canterbury
itself, however, is approachable only by busy roads, so it
does not feature in these routes, though anyone choosing to
stay at Wye (Routes 5 and 7) or Chilham (Route 7) is
only a short train journey from the city.

Kent has many celebrated great houses and lovely
gardens. Again, many of them unfortunately lie on heavily
used main roads. However, the routes do pass by or within
a few miles of three examples: Sissinghurst and Scotney
Castle (Route 6), and Godmersham Park – where Jane
Austen stayed – in Route 7. Route 6 includes a visit to the
superbly sited monastic ruins of Bayham Abbey, and
Route 5 begins (and could easily be extended to end) at
Rye . . . though Rye, of course, is over the border again,
in Sussex.

Neither accommodation nor transport will pose problems
in Kent. Most villages and all larger towns have inns and
bed-and-breakfast places. The railway network irritates
commuters, with its lack of direct routes and fast trains
and its idiosyncracies (Canterbury has two stations on two
lines, a mile apart) – a legacy of the days when rival
companies operated rival services. However, the lack of
high-speed links need not inconvenience holiday-making
cyclists. On the contrary, there is a pleasant choice of rural
routes. Ashford is linked to both Canterbury and Rye (the
latter line, used in Route 5, narrowly escaped Beeching's
axe). North of the railway via Tunbridge Wells to
Hastings, from which two of the rides start, another line

from London runs via Tonbridge to Ashford. This, too,
includes rural stations, which you might use to shorten or
adapt Route 7 – or from which you might set out on
Kentish travels into places which I have never visited.

Route 5:
Romney Marsh and the Downs

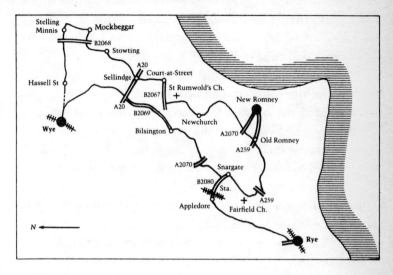

Rye to Appledore (or Rye circular)

This route, easy riding for the most part, crosses four
distinct geological regions: marsh, sand and clay,
escarpment, plateau. We begin and end on Romney
Marsh. Between the levels and the chalk downland lies a
belt of undulating clay, unspectacular country, with some
dullish stretches. Later, beyond Hassell Street, comes a
pleasant open plateau. Climbing the scarp up onto this
chalk, through the valleys and quiet hills east of Wye, you
are in scenery as gently but insistently memorable as any
in the south-east. I love this corner. Wye, Olantigh Park,
Crundale, Pett Street, Hassell Street: the names have
become emblems of the landscape, which I always miss
when a year has gone by without my seeing it.

Returning in springtime in 1990, I found the woods

ravaged by the fierce New Year winds. Yellow earthmovers laboured over the bare soil, zig-zagging between huge stranded trunks, crushing and piling boughs and brushwood. The sharp smoke of green beech drifted in the lanes. An articulated lorry, 'Globetrotter' emblazoned on its cab, confronted us, incongruously, in the tracks and No Through Roads above Wye. But the charm of the landscape still came through. I was delighted to be back ... despite the cold (we camped out on what proved, we were assured the next day, to have been the coldest night for three years). Watching the moon rise through beech boughs, sitting on a low grassy ridge far from the roads, Geoff and I were certainly glad of the huge fire we had built.

We pass through this same district, and explore more of Kent's chalk slopes and plateaux, in Route 7. Here, we approach the downs across Romney Marsh, perhaps Kent's best-known landscape feature (excepting, I suppose, Dover Cliffs). I had ridden up the western fringe of the Marsh before: how, I wondered, would I characterise this wide stretch of reclaimed land when once I had got to know it a little better? We rode back south-west across the heart of it, stopping to look at a couple of the many historic churches whose towers rise, visible for miles, above the flatness. 'Wild', 'remote'? – no, it was neither. 'Bleak' it certainly would be, in the wet or under lowering cloud. And there is something scruffy, provisional, transitory about many of the buildings, most of them (it seems) anonymously post-1945: unpretentious but usually ugly bungalows, small red-brick estates in the villages, hangar-like modern barns and machine sheds and warehouses. Still, plenty of open space remains. The Marsh does keep an idiosyncratic character, pre-modern if not primeval: emptiness and wide sky. For us, this came out intermittently – most strongly and with most appeal in the last miles of our ride, as we followed very quiet lanes, with views south over the dead flat land to the sea, towards the timber-framed church of St Thomas à Becket at Fairfield.

Rye to Appledore (or Rye circular)

Distance: 80 miles. OS 189

Duration: Two days (one or two overnight stops)

Terrain: Much of the route is flat or very flat. But there are some climbs, most of them short, which will make gears worthwhile. East of Wye, paths and tracks run into the Downs. In wet weather, and after it, these tracks will be sticky, but it is easy to find a route on lanes between Wye and Hassell Street.

Itinerary: Trains to **Rye** from London Charing Cross and Waterloo, via either Hastings or Ashford.

Follow the main Tonbridge road (A268) out of Rye across the railway bridge, but turn off right before leaving town on lane signposted to Appledore. Follow the Royal Military Canal NE all the way to the classified road, which you must take E to Appledore station. Beyond the station take first left, then right to lane junction at grid ref. 990297. Turn right here, then next left, riding just E of N to meet the classified A2070. Take this right, then take next lane left. At T-junction turn left, then fork right and ride NE to **Bilsington** (grid ref. 040344) (17 miles).

Follow classified road NE out of Bilsington, forking left up the B2069 at the fork, and crossing the railway and the M20. Ride through Smeeth and Brabourne Lees (grid ref. 080403) towards Brabourne and the lane marked 'Pilgrims' Way', which you join at grid ref. 102422. Follow this lane NW along the foot of the scarp to the lane junction at grid ref. 066465, just above **Wye** (31 miles).

Access to the Downs above Wye and Crundale is by a variety of lanes, tracks and bridleways: there are also footpaths if you want to leave your bicycle and walk. Our route picks up metalled lanes again just past **Hassell Street** (grid ref. 090465) (35 miles).

From the lane crossroads at grid ref. 096463, ride just N of E to cross the B2068 and so to Stelling Minnis (grid ref. 144467). Taking lane SE, turn right at lane junction and so almost due S to Mockbeggar (grid ref. 149438). Double back NW to cross the B2068 and follow lanes to Stowting Common (grid ref. 124434) and Stowting, where head in network of lanes SW to **Sellindge** (grid ref. 094385) (50 miles).

Ride S out of Sellindge on the lane across railway and motorway, reaching the B2067 at Court-at-Street. Ride W as far as the lane turn-off at grid ref. 053352. Follow this lane down onto the Marsh, crossing the canal just below **St Rumwold's church** (58 miles).

From here a wide choice of routes on lanes will take you SW to either Rye or Appledore. We went via Newchurch (grid ref. 054314) and by lanes just W of S to where the lane joins the classified road at grid ref. 039264, between Ivychurch and New Romney. Detouring to see the ruins of Hope Church (grid ref. 049257), we returned to the lane junction (grid ref. 039264) and turned left for **Old Romney** (69 miles).

Just NW of Old Romney, at grid ref. 029253, take the lane left off the A259. Take first right and then first left to lane junction at grid ref. 009239. Here turn right and keep as far as possible to the SW. At grid ref. 978245 you join the main road very briefly, turning off left at once. Ride NW to the church by the lane at Fairfield (grid ref. 966265). From here ride via either Appledore village or Snargate to **Appledore Station** (grid ref. 975298) (80 miles).

From Appledore station there are trains to London via either Rye and Hastings or Ashford.

Rye is in Sussex, a couple of miles from the Kent boundary. It is much visited by sightseers, and justifiably so. It was an important Cinque Port, and its rich history (well documented and surveyed for the Tudor period in Graham Mayhew's *Tudor Rye*) is very much part of its attraction. This history is still clearly visible, thanks to Rye's exceptionally well-preserved condition. It has expanded only a little beyond its original site on a hill rising from the floodplain, and most of the buildings on the knoll date back 200 years and more.

Climb by cobbled streets to St Mary's church, the Ypres Tower and the little town museum. From up here, wide views open out – inland to the faint line of the Downs, away east over the Marsh, down the meanders of the Rother by Rye harbour to the sea. South-east, against the cold-looking Channel, the nuclear power station stands four-square, concrete, on the shingle spit at Dungeness. Just after the Second World War, Richard Church described Dungeness as remote, eccentric. Its people walked the shifting beach on boards tied to their boots. Something called the 'Dungeness cart' would brave the shingle, too, with foot-wide felloes to its wheels. None of this can survive now. Military danger areas flank the site of the power station. Pylons stride confidently away inland. Riding out of the Marsh or dropping down into it, cycling in the lanes by Old Romney, you will see the massive reactor houses outlined against the sea haze. Our road over the levels switched back and forth under the high tension lines, and across the little rural-seeming railtrack along which nuclear waste is taken via Ashford and London to Sellafield/Windscale. But I shall not mention any of this again here.

Arrive early in Rye, or begin this trip with a night spent there, and you will have time to wander about, see the sights, have something to eat (no town, surely can have a higher quota of pubs and teashops and cafés and wine bars . . .). After an earlyish lunch, head north-east alongside the Royal Military Canal, which bears the distinction – not such a rare distinction – of having roused Cobbett to one of his displays of ire:

> Here is a Canal . . . made for the length of thirty miles . . . to *keep out the French*: for those armies who had so often crossed the Rhine

and the Danube, were to be kept back by a canal, made by Pitt, thirty feet wide at the most.

To the left of your road rise sandstone bluffs, where the last of the Wealden ridge (paralleling the South Downs by Eastbourne and the North Downs by Dover) once met the sea. The bluffs are still cliff-like in their exposed, sudden fall. Trees clothe their foot and here and there among these stand cottages and houses. Towards Appledore is a particularly fine house, of the eighteenth century I would guess (and half-spoiled by a foolish inconsequential modern addition), roofed with slate and with distinctive ornate Dutch gable-ends.

This flat and easy run (easy unless you meet a headwind) makes an introduction to the Marsh. For now, swinging north and east a little beyond Appledore, we are heading inland, for the chalk hills. To get there, you cross a rather indeterminate landscape. Geologically this lies between the alluvial soil of the reclaimed levels and the chalk downs. It is mixed sand and clay, and the scarp which rises beyond it is mantled in periglacial deposits:

> The marly Lower Chalk occupies the footslope of the North Downs where it is often obscured by colluvium (hill-wash) and Coombe Deposits (chalky sludge) created during the tundra conditions which prevailed in Kent during the Ice Ages. . . . Above a boundary coinciding almost exactly with the Pilgrims' Way, the Middle Chalk, purer, whiter and with a few flints near the top, makes up most of the scarp and crest of the Downs.
>
> (Burnham and McRae, *Kent: The Garden of England*)

An hour or so after climbing away from the Marsh, you will reach the Pilgrims' Way, which here runs along a quiet lane round the foot of the scarp. It was pleasant to be clear of the rather anonymous modern settlements of Bilsington and Bonnington and Aldington and Brabourne Lees – and to be beyond the trunk road, its six lanes worn glossy by the flood of cars and trucks, whose tyres fill the air with a soulless whizzing and humming for miles around.

The day, cold but blue earlier, had clouded over. Five miles away, the grim office blocks of Ashford stood in stormy, white-and-yellow light under a bitter north-west wind. As we swung beneath the scarp, with wide views through leafless trees and bushes beside the lane, snow began to fall, big flakes, dry and feathery.

The date was 4th April. I was glad to have my woolly hat and quilted jacket. Geoff was pleased that his new hi-tech thermal vest, a present from his father-in-law, was proving quite effective. He was glad he had brought his gloves – I was very sorry I had left mine at home. Thinking of the night ahead, we wondered how cold it would be in tents above Crundale . . . (if we had been less hardy, we could have found accommodation in pubs or B and Bs at Wye or Hassell Street). Shouldn't we have heeded the sound advice of Kate – 'Take *two* sleeping bags, Mart, and put one inside the other' – and Nannette – 'Wouldn't a hot water bottle be a sensible idea?'

At Wye, where there are several buildings associated with the College, we spent a while looking for a water tap. A man in the Pig Research Unit helpfully directed us to the workers' messroom. There, beneath colour photos of pigs pinned to the noticeboard, we filled our water bottles. And now, as we climbed a dead-end lane up towards the empty downland, the snow stopped and a welcome, wintry sunlight filtered through branches onto the road surface. There were storm-felled trees everywhere: it was here that we saw JCBs and came up head-on against the Globetrotter. But the sunlight strengthened, the pure air was radiant, and despite the cold our hearts rose.

We pitched our tents where a bridle path ran along the edge of a wood, and out on a low ridge between ploughlands. To the west, beyond wooded hollows near at hand, across the valley of the Great Stour above Ashford, we saw forested downs rising into the last evening light. To the east the ploughed field dipped, brown and flinty, to a cluster of farm buildings in the valley floor, and then narrow pasture slopes separated by strips of wood rose abruptly to the starry sky. The next day dawned sunny, freezing: ice had formed in the kettle. The sun soon reached the grass by our tents, and warmed us as we drank tea and ate boiled eggs, but the white frost was still lying on those sunless slopes when, at mid-morning, riding past the Woodman's Arms at Hassell Street, we found ourselves back on metalled lanes.

This next day was for the Marsh, really, and for the Marsh churches, or as many of them as it proved pleasant to stop and look at. First came a zig-zag run across the chalk plateau, large fields and strips of copse, spring corn under the chilly blue sky.

Not far beyond Hassell Street a young man whizzed past us on an unladen bike. Chafe, chafe, chafe: his wildly buckled rear wheel caught at the brakeblocks. A couple of hundred yards on, he stopped (at the foot of a climb), flung his machine onto the verge, and attempted brutally to straighten out the kinked rim by jumping up and down on it.

'There's the photo,' said Geoff, 'for the cover of your book.'

Coming up to him, we commiserated, and offered the loan of tools. He did not want any. The one thing he was looking forward to, he explained, in connection with this bicycle, was the moment when he would take a sledgehammer to it. It was a good frame, he assured us, an Eddie Merckx, but unfortunately – he pointed to the down tube just above the bottom bracket – it had had to be welded. Also, the pedals came off all the time: he plucked one easily, by way of demonstration. He did have another bike at home: it was better than this one, in the sense that it was not mechanically ruinous, but on the other hand it was far too small. Anyway: he was off to work, if he could only get there.

'I'm glad to say', he added, 'that today I'll be digging my last fence-post hole.'

'Hard work, isn't it,' Geoff sympathised. 'You can see why they invented a machine to do it.'

And so through Stelling Minnis, where two goats browsed outside the sleepy-looking lace-curtained police station, and across part of that scattered woodland known collectively as Lyminge Forest (the patch we crossed was coniferous, edged with broadleaf), and to Sellindge. Here, in the church, I successfully identified a piece of Geoff's work, a memorial plaque for which he had cut the letters. A while later we dropped past another church, dedicated to St Rumwold, down onto the Marsh.

Its sudden edge – like sea meeting land, as indeed sea did once meet land all along here – is one of Romney Marsh's characteristics. The Royal Military Canal emphasises this clean-edged quality, running from Rye round to Hythe at the periphery of the reclaimed land.

The canal now forms part of the network of drainage channels that keep the Marsh dry. Indeed 'marsh' is no name, nowadays, for most of these fields. Their dark dry earth is increasingly given over to arable crops, and it has become a region as much of corn and yellow, garish rapeseed as of sheep. The Romney Marsh breed is still famous, and still in evidence, but the days are over (at least for the time being) when all this was one great sheepwalk. Something of the landscape's former uniqueness and apartness (the guidebook in St Clement's, Old Romney, quotes a reference to this as 'the fifth quarter of the globe') ebbed away, no doubt, as mechanised ploughing and sowing and spraying and cropping took over. And the pylons have come, of course, and the motor cars.

However, the lanes were quiet on this early April weekday. In summer, when trippers to the sands and holiday villages at Dymchurch and Camber drive back inland for a look at the Marsh they probably keep to the A and B roads, so there may well be quiet lanes on the Marsh even in July and August.

By the canal, below St Rumwold's, we ate lunch: lazy-looking yellow light, but the air was cool, and hot soup was welcome (a word of praise for Geoff's primus: dangerous in unskilled hands, maybe, but three times as fast as gas stoves). Then we snaked south and west and back north, between the hedges of ash and alder and willow, along below the embanked watercourse of White Kemp Sewer which marks the seaward limit of the inland roads and settlements. Looking from here over to the ribbon of holiday development at Camber, which is fortunately invisible below the dykes, you seen only bare fields, sheepwalks mostly. Back inland, the churches, almost the only buildings (or so it seems to a passing cyclist) with any historic character, rise from what looks like an empty landscape.

We visited three churches – or rather three sites, for the first, the ruins of Hope Church near New Romney, is nothing now but a collapsed framework, a skeleton of rubble, its lime cement crumbling inexorably away. Geoff explained how it would have been built, with quicklime slaked on-site to make the mortar, and how it had fallen apart as the marshland subsided. In broad daylight, a hundred yards from the main road, it was not so very atmospheric: but a farmer who came across to talk (and who told us that he had that morning fetched his sheep back from winter grazing in West Sussex) assured us that 'some of the old boys put their tents up here', and – as well as wondering who these 'old boys' might be, and whether we might be in that category – I imagined the site at dusk, with the sun sinking over Rye and a wind creeping off the sea. Then it might be desolate enough.

Fairfield Church, almost at the end of our ride, was in a quieter spot. But the building has been much restored since the nineteenth century and looks unromantic, though its unusual timber framing gives it archaeological interest.

The most rewarding visit was to the Church of St Clement at Old Romney. Here, modern restoration has been carried out with skilful unobtrusiveness – not before time, for there was a move to declare the building redundant. The old tie-beams running across the airy nave were strengthened, and the fine eighteenth-century minstrels' gallery, a rare survival, was made safe. There is interesting stonework, including a fourteenth-century font, Purbeck marble of the Decorated period. A guidebook by Anne Roper, FSA, gives an account of church and village and medieval Romney Marsh. After enjoying the cool, airy church – the pure light of sea and sky pours in through the windows' clear glass – we sat against the sunlit west wall, drinking tea and writing postcards, sheltered from the wind, basking, getting warm for the last scenic stretch of riding to Fairfield and Appledore station and the train home.

Route 6:
Weald, Orchards and Bayham Abbey

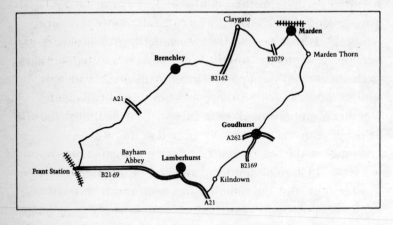

Frant circular

This route takes you through typically Kentish scenes.
Dropping past Brenchley, with its busy traffic and new
housing, you find yourself suddenly in quiet country beside
the Teise. Good, light soils overlie the Wealden clay. The
land is divided between cornfields, orchards and hop
gardens, a flat and wide-skied patchwork, deeply peaceful
once you ride a little eastwards, delightful at blossom-time.
Easy going, too, for the cyclist. Climbing back to
Goudhurst, and from there over to Kilndown, you must
work harder, but fine views reward you: pastures and big
woods set on rolling slopes, with hazy prospects
northwards across the orchard country to the hills by
Maidstone.

This is a comfortable day's ride for a reasonably fit
cyclist (I left Frant station just before midday and was
back at six). You could stay overnight at Tunbridge Wells,
before or after the trip, or you could break your journey at

Goudhurst. That way, with a more relaxed schedule, you would have time for all the monuments and parklands lying on or just off the route. I visited Bayham Abbey, and glimpsed Scotney Castle. Within half a dozen miles east and south of Goudhurst are Sissinghurst gardens, and Angley Wood below Cranbrook, and Bedgebury woods and pinetum just east of the Flimwell road. You can reach all of these, circuitously, by B roads and lanes. Sissinghurst and Cranbrook can also be reached more directly, but much less safely and pleasantly, east from Goudhurst along the A262.

Angley and Bedgebury, traversed by footpaths and (in the latter case) bridleways, tempt you off your bike to plunge into deep woods. In fine summer weather under thick leaves, you will find that seclusion among sylvan scents and sounds which is one of southern England's special gifts. Seclusion is epitomised at Bayham Abbey, too. But it is not the only keynote of this ride. From time to time, crossing busy A roads or following them for a mile, coming suddenly on the press of tourists at Goudhurst or of commuter traffic pouring at rush hour out of the station car park at Frant or Wadhurst, you will be reminded of Kent's exposure to the pressures of modernity. These contrasts, between country and suburbia, lanes and trunk roads, silence and noise, are as pronounced as the contrast between the flat riverside orchards and the steep and wooded High Weald.

Frant circular

Distance: 40 miles. OS 188

Duration: Day trip

Terrain: The part of the route lying in orchard country is flat, but the Wealden stretches include some stiff and sometimes longish climbs. Low gears are needed and even then many riders will prefer to get off and push. *Note*: near Lamberhurst, the A21, which can be very busy, is unavoidably followed for just under 2 miles. For that reason this route is not suitable for younger riders.

Itinerary: Trains to **Frant** (one stop beyond Tunbridge Wells) from London Charing Cross, Waterloo East and London Bridge.

On leaving Frant station (grid ref. 606364), turn right along main road, then left at first crossroads down lane signposted to Hawkenbury and Kipping's Cross. At crossroads just over a mile on, turn right and through the valley to Kipping's Cross on the A21 (grid ref. 645400). Then either via the B2160 or via lanes just E of it to **Brenchley** (grid ref. 675418) (8 miles).

From Brenchley follow lanes just N of E to join the B2162 at Ram's Hill (grid ref. 707422). Ride just E of N to Claygate. Here, take lane on right to ride SE to Marden Beech (grid ref. 738432). Cross the main road and ride towards Marden, but turn right at T-junction and double back SE to Marden Thorn (grid ref. 760431). Ride S on lanes towards Blantyre House (grid ref. 755402), turning right to head W and SW on lanes to **Goudhurst** (20 miles).

Leave Goudhurst S on the B2079, taking first right less than 1 mile out of the village and so on lanes SW via Kilndown to the A21 at grid ref. 694341. Take the A road NW for just under 2 miles, forking off left on the B2169 as you enter Lamberhurst. Continue just N of W on the B2169 to the entrance drive to **Bayham Abbey** (at grid ref. 648359). After visiting the abbey return to the main road and ride W to **Frant station** (40 miles).

Frant station has an attractive Victorian ticket office. To my untrained eye, it appeared to be built of local sandstone, used in so many of the Wealden churches. It was in 1851 that the South Eastern Railway first reached out beyond Tunbridge Wells with what Hardy calls its 'steam feeler'; at least when it came it showed some concern for local styles and traditions. . . . Dropping down from the village and then climbing back up, a characteristic Wealden swoop and push, you are in extensive private woodlands. Pleasant, rural riding at the start of your trip.

Then comes the A21, with heavy traffic. All these Wealden ridges are usurped by major roads; they have magnificent long views, but are inhospitable to the cyclist. Fortunately we need not spend any time on the A21, and are soon in Brenchley.

Brenchley, however, is no longer the 'enchanting village' mentioned in Richard Church's volume *Kent* in the 'County Books' series (and celebrated, Church reminds us, in Siegfried Sassoon's autobiography). Successive waves of development have largely submerged its original character. Entering the village, I passed two estate agents' offices – not much help in my search for tea bags and apples:

Brenchley, Kent, lunchtime, 23 April 1990

Brenchley . . . village with two estate agents and no shop? That's what I thought when I arrived. Now, having found the Stores, I'm sitting on a bench eating, on a little green. Busy road – though marked as a lane on my OS. Opposite me chugs the diesel engine of a parked articulated lorry, Sittingbourne Car Breakers, with a broken car duly aboard. The driver, who'd stopped to buy cigarettes, throws a match out of the cab window and pulls away in a cloud of exhaust, to reveal the Bull Inn of Brenchley. They advertise their 'completely refurbished Victorian Barn' as a venue for Private Functions.

In short, despite the sandstone church reached by its alley of clipped yews, this is not yet the countryside. I *have* seen fields of appleblossom (and of course I have already crossed lovely slopes of the Weald, too). And there's flowering cherry blooming pinkly – too pinkly? – everywhere. . . . On to Ram's Hill, and Claygate, and the valley of the Teise.

East out of Brenchley, you soon come to a fine prospect down over the orchard country. There is a considerately placed bench, should you want to stop and enjoy the view. (This would be a better place than Brenchley Green for a

bite to eat.) Cars were still fairly frequent until I left the
B road at Claygate . . . then, riding easily along flat Sheep-
hurst Lane, I was suddenly in quiet, even sleepy country.

Hops and apples, apples and hops. The uniformity of
this horticulture may pall on the local people, I suppose,
but if you come from town or more ordinary farming
landscape you will find charm enough in the repeated rows
of trees, wheeling past geometrically, hypnotically, and in
the unfamiliar sight of hop gardens with their poles and
aerial wirework. When I passed, the plants had barely
begun growing back after winter's suspended animation. In
some fields it looked as if poles were still being strung, in
others men seemed already to be training the growing
bines around the supports. Hop cultivation involves far
more hand labour than growing wheat or barley. But it is
clearly still an economic proposition – beer, after all, goes
on being drunk – for there were many fields newly given
over to this very traditional Kentish crop.

The other traditional crop is, of course, fruit, especially
apples. There were orchards in every stage of growth, from
tiny saplings protected by plastic sheaths to tough-looking
old trees, their trunks surrounded by boughs lopped off at
pruning or blown off by storms. These neatly stacked
woodpiles were for firewood, no doubt: they made me
think of sweet, hot campfires in the orchards of Normandy.
Modern growers prefer trees not more than eight or ten
feet tall. The older trees, many-branched, at once wild-
looking and dignified, have mostly been replaced by closely
pruned plants that make cropping easier. However, as I
climbed away from the fruit zone into the wooded slopes
that overlook it, I did see one image that might have been
paralleled any time these last hundred years: sheep let into
an orchard of fine old trees, grazing on the undergrass.

This southern extension of the mid-Kent fruit belt is

watered by the Teise, which (like that other orchard-river, the Beult, beyond Marden and the Tonbridge–Ashford railway) drains into the Medway. A couple of miles below Horsmonden, the Teise rather oddly divides in two. The westerly stream flows directly to the Medway at Yalding, while the other branch joins the Beult near Benover. I left my bike at the end of a cornfield and followed a footpath to look at this curious parting of the waters. It seemed to me that, but for a simple earthwork of rocks and timber, the westerly stream would have been starved of its supply. Presumably by dividing the headwaters, Kentish growers have irrigated a larger area of this rather dry region? But in hydrology, as in much else, my curiosity outruns my expertise. It was certainly a lovely place for a picnic!

Teise banks, 2.00pm, 23 April 1990

Green, cold-looking river water divides in front of me, where I sit in sun and breeze on the bank, cornfield behind me. The eastern stream tumbles musically over its weir/stepping stones. It eddies tumbling under the far bank, cutting into the soft sandy earth. From the woods across the river – where the leaves are out on the hazels, budding on the willows, and still closed on the wintry ash – comes the strong smell of wild garlic. Birdsong and the tumbling of the water are the only sounds.

Climbing towards Goudhurst, you are back in the High Weald. We saw it at the beginning of this ride and shall see it again in East Sussex (Routes 9 and 10). Goudhurst church's square ragstone tower stands pleasingly on this northernmost ridge of the high ground. The village has typical Wealden character, with its tile-hung and weatherboarded houses, its newer dwellings clinging to the steep slopes below the original nucleus, and its over-busy main road. Less typical – positively surprising at this height – is the pond which stands beside the road south. Church, pond, attractive houses, nice pubs, and a teashop or two:

little wonder that pretty Goudhurst was attracting its
complement of tourists even on a Monday in mid-April. I
would like best to be there on a fine autumn evening, with
the crowds gone, the road quiet, and woodsmoke.
However, its attractive buildings, and the wonderful views
you will enjoy as you ride out of it, make it a place to visit
at any season.

As attractive, almost, as Goudhurst, but less obviously
so (and for that reason far less crowded), is Kilndown, just
a couple of miles to the south. A lovely, strenuous, up-and-
down lane brings you gasping to the Globe Inn and the
church behind it – a sandstone church, early Victorian I
would guess, with some pleasant grotesque carving. The
village is recent rather than ancient: nineteenth century,
with some modern additions, but still compact – as yet. Its
situation makes it memorable and gives it a wonderful
feeling of health and altitude. If I had to convince a friend
of the marvellous qualities of the Wealden landscape, and
had to name just one place in illustration, Kilndown might
be my choice. It has the long, hazily-lit views, the
juxtaposition of pasture and thick copse, and the tumbling,
stream-threaded hillsides which delight the eye.

Kilndown has the merit, too, of being close to
Bedgebury Park and Scotney Castle. At Bedgebury,
footpaths and bridleways lead into a secluded parkland of
trees, grassy slopes and ornamental water. Right below
Kilndown, in the most secret of the valleys which falls
away on three sides of the village, lies Scotney Castle with
its celebrated gardens. The main entrance is off the
Lamberhurst road (we pass it later), but from Kilndown
you can follow footpaths through woods, mostly well-grown
conifers, down into the silent water-meadow. The great
house, built in the early nineteenth century, stands on the
far bank, but the original castle, ruinous now, is visible

right at the river's edge. This is still the Teise, which finds
its way through the ridge just west of Goudhurst.

Still further upstream, and in a site of unparalleled
tranquillity and grace, is Bayham Abbey. It is little
wonder that both Kent and Sussex should wish to lay
claim to this memorable place (the county boundary runs
literally yards from the ruins). In his historical guide, *The
Sussex Landscape*, Peter Brandon refers to Bayham Abbey as
'the most inaccessible of all' the solitary Wealden sites
sought out by twelfth- and thirteenth-century monasticism,
and adds that its buildings form 'an impressive group by
far the most complete and instructive of the Sussex
monastic sites'. Richard Church, implicitly claiming
Bayham for Kent, concludes his description by noting that
'it is a remarkable thing that this solitude can be found,
with such substantial recollections of the medieval world,
within fifty miles of London, and only a mile or two from
the main London to Hastings road.'

These remarkable juxtapositions have been part of
Kent's fabric since the nineteenth century. Travelling from
the remoteness of Scotney Castle to the remoteness of
Bayham Abbey, one has little choice but to ride for two
long miles along that 'main London to Hastings road', the
busy A21. Then after Lamberhurst, itself traffic-ridden,
you must keep on a B road to the abbey gatehouse. The
little lanes which used to loop south of Lamberhurst and
make it possible to cut out some of this have gone,
swallowed up by the rising waters of the Bewl when the
water authority dammed it to make the extensive, pretty
reservoir at Bewl Bridge. And the very last stretch of
riding, back on the B road into Frant, may unnerve you –
though it is not really unpleasant – after Bayham's
serenity.

The abbey's fabric of warm sandstone is aesthetically as well as archaeologically noteworthy, though much damaged. However, it is not the building itself so much as the harmony between building and setting which makes it hard to leave. One wants to stay until sunset; to stay, at any rate, long after one has finished examining the stones and reading the epitaphs and browsing in the English Heritage handbook. There is no more tourism to do. You have looked again and again across the rising ground to the really magnificent nineteenth-century mansion, built for the Marquis of Camden ('this great and awful sinecure placeman', Cobbett calls him) by the architect David Brandon, who restored Chilham Castle (Route 7). But you are still reluctant to leave these oakwoods, these cornfields, this string of pools made from the trickling Teise.

Route 7:

From the Weald of Kent to the North Downs

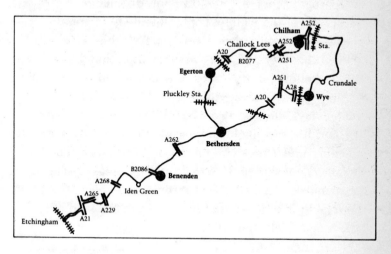

Etchingham circular

This circular tour gives an excellent cross-section of the landscapes of south and mid-Kent: high and low weald, greensand hills, chalk downs. At around ninety miles, it is a substantial two days' ride for a fit cyclist (though the central parts on the flat clay are easy going). But it is a very adaptable route. Additional overnight stays could well be included – at Wye, or (taking the train from Wye or Chilham to avoid the inhospitable A28) at Canterbury. You pass railway stations at Pluckley and Wye and Chilham, so the tour can easily be cut short. You might begin and end at Pluckley, leaving out the southern half. If you draw out the itinerary on the two OS maps, you will see that it can readily be modified.

The entire ride, however, is a delight. The High Weald and North Downs I already knew from earlier expeditions

into Kent and around East Sussex. Wye and Chilham and
Egerton I remembered with much affection. What I had
not anticipated (though a close look at the map might
have prepared me) was the tranquil, distinctive
atmosphere of the watery, copse-dotted sheep country
either side of Bethersden. I say 'watery': this is the
impermeable clay and there are dozens of small ponds and
pools in hollows, and clumps of rushes stand in the fields.
But the weather was anything but watery. I had two
glorious days, the last two days of April, with cloudless
skies and hot sun, high summer warmth, dry dusty gravel
crunching under my tyres on the dappled lanes. The kind
air bathed my skin and poured into my lungs. I sang
louder and louder as I rolled through the green
countryside, I could hardly bear to stop, the land felt
endless and I felt immortal.

Etchingham circular

Distance: 87 miles. OS 188, 189

Duration: Two days (but the route can easily be modified)

Terrain: Steep hills (including some longish hauls) between
Etchingham and Biddenden, and again after Wye. Here you will
probably get off and push. The central section of the route is flat
and easy. The North Downs Way between Chilham and Soakham
will be impassable in winter and after heavy rain: an alternative
route on lanes is given in the itinerary.

Itinerary: Trains to **Etchingham** from London Charing Cross,
Waterloo East and London Bridge.
   Leave Etchingham NE on the A265, and so (via lanes N of the
main road if preferred) to Hurst Green. Turn left on the A21 and

then after less than 1 mile right on the A265 again, forking right on the lane at grid ref. 738282. Take this lane E, cross the A229, and swing NE to the fork at Little Conghurst (grid ref. 773293). Take the left fork and cross the A268, continuing NNE to Scullsgate Farm (grid ref. 792235). Here turn right, and then left at crossroads in Iden Green. Cross the B2086 just W of Benenden. Take the right fork at grid ref. 806342. Ride NE, ignoring turnings off, to reach the edge of this OS sheet at grid ref. 850369. Join the A262, ride N for less than 1 mile, then take the lane to the right and ride ENE to **Bethersden** (grid ref. 930400) (22 miles).

From Bethersden take lanes NE through the southern part of Hoad's Wood to cross the railway at grid ref. 968429. Ride NE to T-junction (grid ref. 978443). Turn right here, and fork right where the lane divides by the new motorway. Ride NE to Lenacre Hall (grid ref. 012459). Take the A251 NE for 1 mile to Boughton Lees. Turn right to cross the A28 and so to **Wye** (grid ref. 055467) (33 miles).

Take the lane that leaves Wye almost due N. Turn right at Olantigh Towers. Ride via Little Olantigh and Crundale village to Crundale church (grid ref. 086486), then via Sole Street to the lane crossroads at grid ref. 101493. Turn left and ride N to Thruxted. Turn left at T-junction to cross the railway at grid ref. 083540, and so into **Chilham** (43 miles).

Leave Chilham on the dead-end lane running just W of S via Mountain Street, which leads into the North Downs Way bridle path. Take this all the way to Soakham Farm and so to the metalled lane at grid ref. 038487. Turn right on lane, join the A251, and so to the crossroads with the A252 at Challock Lees. Either on the A252 or on loops of lane just to the S and then the N, ride W to the lane turn-off at grid ref. 991503, and take the lane right, to Monkery Farm. (*Alternative route avoiding use of bridle path*: From Chilham, take the lane WNW to Shottenden (grid ref. 045543), and bear WSW to cross the A251 and join the B2077 at grid ref. 009531. Follow this B road to Monkery Farm.) At Monkery Farm, take the B road briefly SW and then turn off right on next lane, riding WNW through turnings to the Bowl Inn public house (grid ref. 950513). From here drop down and ride SW via Charing Heath to **Egerton** (grid ref. 906474) (58 miles).

From Egerton, drop down SW, take left at T-junction, and ride SE via Pluckley station (grid ref. 922433) to **Bethersden** (65 miles).

From Bethersden, follow outward route in reverse direction to **Etchingham** (87 miles) for trains to London.

Crossing the main Hastings–Hawkhurst road a few miles out of Etchingham, you are in Kent; but still in the High Weald, which Kent shares with East Sussex. If you want a perfect image of the green and hidden hollows of this Wealden landscape – a stream valley with steep sides and patches of woodland, abrupt ridges closing off the bowl of sky – you might stop (as I did, on my way back at the end of this trip) between Scullsgate Farm and Iden Green. I propped my bike against a gate and took my picnic into the field, which fell away steeply and then rose to the edge of a wood. Trees bordered the grass where I sat, their twigs and new leaves tapping and rustling in the breeze. The drone of insects, birdsong, and the whispering of growth itself as the sap rises and the buds break: was it that complex harmonious murmuring which John Clare had at the back of his mind when he wrote 'And even silence found a tongue / To haunt me all the summer long' ... .? Summer – but there is no such thing, strictly, in the Wealden hills, as a clear day. When the sky above is blue, in whatever season, the earth exhales a pearly mist: it rises to veil the ridges with a soft aura, milky and cool at dawn and in winter, golden when the days grow warm. Haziness suits the layered quality of the views, giving a sense of a repetition that might be infinite as one ridge rises behind another. This complex layering makes these hills quite different from the one bare ridge of the South Downs in East Sussex, and different too from the North Downs near Wye, where, after the abrupt and complex escarpment, the chalk opens into a wide uncomplicated plateau.

This lane by Scullsgate Farm, the lane from Four Throws to Iden Green – narrow, bumpy, little-used – is paralleled a mile to the west by a broader lane marked 'Roman Road'. Lane breadth is indicated, if you look closely, on the OS maps. I would always choose the narrower of two otherwise equal alternatives: the wider the road, the more it intrudes on the landscape, and the busier, especially in the south-east, it is likely to be. After Iden Green, running across the edge of Hemsted Forest by Benenden hospital to the Biddenden road, you are on some of these wider lanes. They were not unduly crowded and the views were good, but I was still glad, swinging east just before Biddenden, to find myself back in remoter and more tranquil country.

You are out of the hills – you have dropped down out of them rather imperceptibly – and over as far as Wye the going is mostly very easy. Westwards, this wide belt of clay is covered with thin deposits of kinder soil around the Teise and Beult rivers, where the orchards and hops grow (Route 6); to the east, it runs to Romney Marsh's north-western borders (Route 5). Hereabouts it supports flocks of sheep and patches of commercial afforestation (such as Hoad's Wood, just before you reach the railway, with its bluebells . . . more of bluebells later). There are copses among the pastures, and generous hedgerows with trees left to grow tall and straggling: shade and shelter for the flocks, and variety for the eye, as your gaze travels over the gently dipping plain, green and calm.

But this is Kent, not Arcadia: corridor Kent, with its high-speed rail link and its upgrading of the Dover roads. Reaching the A20 at Potter's Corner was like waking from a sweet dream. Three minutes' wait before I could cross *that*! Then, beyond it, the wide scar of raw earth, the prefabricated bridge units and yellow machines and the cheerful navvies of the highway engineers, where the parallel route was under construction. A rough patch, aesthetically, but mostly negotiable on lanes. You leave Ashford on your right. Dreaming in haze, which softened the outlines of its tower blocks and gas-holder, the town was lost in summer: four weeks earlier, passing it on the east, I had seen it through snow under winter light.

Below the Downs, north of Wye, by the Great Stour; then up, stiffly, and down, and up, by Crundale with its tiny downland church. This is the sudden-falling, tightly folded and secret landscape of the escarpment. Its shaded lanes look over the slopes to flat pastures by the river, or else into the heart of the chalk, down the long sleepy valleys of Crundale House and Pett Street and Marriage Farm.

There were parked cars and walkers by Crundale church. Wanting solitude, I rode on a couple of hundred yards before stopping to make tea in the shade of woods by the lane. This was only my second stop in thirty-five miles or so, yet I was almost loath to make it: why couldn't I just go drifting on, rolling on? Even the steep climbs seemed a kind of upward drifting, at the slow pace I was taking them, pushing my bike through the warm, murmuring afternoon. . . . But the rest and the hot tea set me up for the day's last climb, up to the crossroads at Sole Street, at 500 feet or so (158 metres). This is the wide plateau, part farmed, part wooded, of the North Downs chalk. No sooner up than down: now you drop gradually, easily, delightfully through forestry woods, by Mystole House (I seem to recall a signboard referring to a newly established vineyard here), across the railway to Chilham.

At the level crossing the crossing-keeper was just sauntering out of his garden gate to shut the barriers behind me. 'Not many of these left,' I said. But he replied that between Ashford and Canterbury there were still quite a few manned crossings. It was an anachronistic touch, making the railway seem (as it often seems) part of the nineteenth century. Yet not far from here they are projecting the new non-stop London–Paris link.

If you are looking for the quintessential English village, then Chilham and Egerton are the two highlights of this ride. Chilham is surprisingly quiet (the main road passes to the north), with pubs and teashops and gift boutiques around the pretty triangular square fronting the castle entrance. The castle has landscaped grounds and a colony of birds of prey which can be seen flying most days of the week in summer. With Canterbury six miles away and the North Downs all around, this is a fine place to visit: continental tourists were strolling under the walls and sitting on shady benches.

I did not stop for tea. Tea I could make (having filled my water container at a tap in the churchyard) up in the woods, where the North Downs Way, following a dead-end lane out of the village and then striking uphill along the boundary of Godmersham Park, runs for three or four miles at the edge of Challock Forest. Tea, and supper, and a night beside the path, on a grassy trackway between beech plantations. Had the weather been ordinary, I would have stayed in Chilham: there is a good selection of B and Bs (book ahead in the high season). But the prospect of putting my tent up under the full-starred sky was irresistible. I must add, however, that you are not meant to camp on Forestry Commission land. Should you be tempted to do so, light no fires, and leave no trace.

North Downs Way, SW of Chilham, 7.00pm, 29 April 1990
The bridleway is dry, if rutted, mostly, though here and there it gets muddy where rainpools have lingered in the shade. But a

runner who passed me just before I stopped assured me that the track is not blocked, ahead, by fallen trees, which had been my worry. So I think I will continue SW on this track tomorrow morning, rather than go back via Chilham.

Perfect evening, faintest sea-breeze. Sun still quite high, and quite warm. There is a murmur of traffic in the Stour valley, and I have just heard – almost a pastoral sound, in comparison – the hoot and rattle of a train on the Ashford–Canterbury line. Close at hand evening insects are buzzing and there is constant birdsong (earlier I heard cuckoos). A dog barks in Godmersham Park, sheep are bleating, pheasants squawk.

Behind me recently cut coppices of beech are regrowing, thriving, and in front of me older standard trees, still immature, twelve or fifteen feet high, are coming into leaf. All day I have been aware of trees, trees, trees: oaks colour of bronze and honey, chestnuts with their candles about to burst into bloom, here and there – in some of the many parklands I have passed – a copper beech. And how many of the woods have been carpeted, as here, with bluebells more hazily intense, more prodigally profuse, than I have ever seen.

Walking, strolling, either way along the track, I gaze clear over the hazy valley to the Downs over by Crundale. The eastern horizon is an almost level ridge, where the plateau ends and the scarp drops suddenly to the Stour. Even the brilliant yellow of one large field of rapeseed is absorbed in the formal harmony of the view. And away to the north-east, catching the last sun from the south-west, rises a massive pale church tower: it can only be Canterbury Cathedral.

So: 'Here I am in Kent and Christendom / Among the Muses . . .': I read some poems of Edward Thomas. Then one last walk. The sun was in the mist above the skyline, still brilliant, reddish now, dropping minute by minute: when I stood up and left my book it was clear of the horizon, when I sat down ten minutes later it was gone. And counterpointing its red glow was the dense haze beneath the beeches where the earth was flooded with bluebells.

★

Next morning I was awake at five (woken by bluebell scent); I had had tea and breakfast and taken down the tent and was on the move by six. Then came an hour of enchanted solitary walking. Morning filled the valley with yellow light and sent long shadows dancing across the dry path. I saw deer and rabbits and smelt sap and earth and bluebells: there were bluebells flooding every patch of cut coppice.

In the last stretch, dropping down to Soakham Farm amidst the ruins of mature beeches, you will see signs of the storm damage so evident in much of Kent. Most of this fine wood, however, seems to have gone unscathed.

At Soakham, a Chaucerian moment, fittingly in the Canterbury district: a swaggering farmyard cock, gaudy, vainglorious, imperturbable – Chauntecleer, striding about his territory. No sign of Pertelote, his paramour and partner, 'courteous and discreet and debonair' – and also gently sardonic, responding to his death-or-glory dreams with the suggestion that he should 'take some laxative'. This cock, at ten past seven on a perfect summer morning, had his walk to himself.

Woods, still, up the long climb to the main road; woods at Challock Lees, where you pass the Forestry Commission offices; woods, and bluebells, and wide grassy verges, and a gang of forestry workers sitting on piled logs and drinking tea and watching their brushwood fire blazing, by the lane to Monkery Farm. 'The North Downs upper dipslope', says my topographical guide, 'shares with the High Weald the distinction of being the most heavily wooded part of Kent.' Now I have sweet memories of that 'upper dipslope' and its coppices.

From the Bowl Inn, you see Egerton church tower, prominent on the crest of the greensand ridge which runs parallel to the scarp of the Downs right across the county. I freewheeled downhill. A brilliant yellowhammer flashed across a field of rapeseed brilliantly in bloom. Then I was down, and across the motorway roadworks, and climbing to Egerton. The church is a fine sight, and its square tower has a typically Kentish feature (found also at Bethersden and Biddenden), an octagonal turret at the north-east corner. This carried a flagpole. It was not difficult to imagine the cross of St George aloft. Letters cut on the First World War memorial read: 'You who live on 'mid English pastures green / Remember us, and think what might have been.' I resist the assimilation of place to nation, and then of nation to Motherland and Fatherland, but Englishness seems to cling sometimes to a place or settle on it.

Better to call Egerton an ordinary, charming village, with a good church and a nice pub and a shop whose proprietor cheerfully filled my water container. He also sold me the materials for a second breakfast, which I ate at a bench on the green. Every village store contains some item which people must count (or it would not justify its share of the limited space available) among life's necessaries, but which I not only do not need, but have never heard of. This morning at Egerton, it was Robin Frend Pre-Wash Spray for Removing Grime from Collars and Cuffs. While I gazed at this commodity, a neighbour rushed in to warn the grocer that the blackbirds were at his grapes again. He sighed and said he would have to cover them up, like yesterday: they always got pecked in the dry weather.

Ordinary, if attractive (its buildings, old and new, are solid and spacious), Egerton might be if it did not have such extraordinary views. From back beyond the church, you look north to the Downs. From the green, and widening out as you begin to drop downhill, is a sweeping prospect across the clay vale towards Bethersden – the sheep and copse country I had cycled through at midday the day before, and would soon be sailing across once more, blown by a breeze of warm air and exhilaration. The blue view melts into nothingness just as the High Weald begins to rise. You have the sense, up at Egerton, of overlooking a new and distinctive region, self-contained, with its own soils and weather (rather like the Vale of Blackmore, as Hardy describes it in *Tess*, seen from the chalk ridge that bounds it). Chalk, greensand, clay, Wealden hills: at Egerton, you have a moment, or an hour, to enjoy the contrasts which are part of the charm of this wonderful ride.

7. East Sussex

The sea, the narrow coastal strip, the famous chalk ridge
of the South Downs, and then the mixed soils of the plain
rising inland towards the High Weald: that, briefly (and a
little over-simply), is East Sussex's topography. A ribbon
of dense housing, bulging up the valleys and encroaching
onto the hills; then, inland of the Downs, mixed arable and
pasture, dotted with commuter towns, lined by straggling
hedges and variegated with patches of copse, criss-crossed
by busy roads; then quieter lanes among steeper fields,
stream valleys, forestry plantations – so the landscape
alters and becomes emptier as you ride north-east. Rivers
pierce the Downs at Lewes and just west of Eastbourne,
and the complex drainage of the Weald finds its chief
outlet in the Rother, flowing to the sea at Rye and
marking, for part of its length, the Kent/Sussex border.
Within this overall pattern, there are distinctive landscapes
at Pevensey Levels and among the woods and open heaths
of Ashdown Forest. The routes described in this chapter
give glimpses of these, as well as pleasant river-plain riding
north of Lewes and miles of exhilarating, if energetic, lanes
in the surprisingly remote High Weald.

The coastal strip is narrow everywhere in East Sussex, and
the ribbon of housing which fronts the sea wherever the
land is flat enough for building generates constant traffic.
Long, or indeed short, stretches of peaceful cycling just

cannot be found here. One fairly quiet road does give access to the shore, however: if you take the train to Berwick (a couple of stops west of Eastbourne), you can ride down the woody Cuckmere valley to the country park at the river mouth, and then along car-free tracks to the sand-and-shingle beach. This is a pleasant trip (quite busy, though, in summer), but it hardly qualifies as a day's cycling.

The Downs are another matter. The obvious solution to the problem of busy roads in southern East Sussex is to get up onto the South Downs Way. A bridle path all its length, it is legally open to cyclists, and the going is for the most part quite firm, though the chalk gets sticky in the rain. By train to Hassocks (on the Brighton line), Falmer (between Lewes and Brighton), Southease (between Lewes and Newhaven) or Berwick, and then by short stretches of lanes or B roads, you can be up on the Way in less than two hours after leaving London. With a mountain bike you will be able to ride most of it at any season; with a touring machine, there will be times and places where pushing seems more sensible. Take it slowly, at all events, and admire the views. The sea is usually in sight across the gentle dip-slope to the south, and hazy prospects stretch inland below the steeply falling escarpment. There will be sheep, though nowhere near as many as in pre-war days, and cows, and ramblers, and other cyclists, but you will feel airily remote from the busy roads below.

I give no routes for the South Downs Way in East Sussex, since it is the subject of several guidebooks and can in any case be followed easily on the OS maps. I certainly advise you to try it: a day or two up on the chalk ridge might well be combined with either Route 8 or Route 10. A word of caution: the Way is very exposed, especially in East Sussex where there are few sheltering trees. Wear warm clothes and take rainproof ones. And make sure you have plenty of drinking water.

The plain that spreads north of the Downs generally lacks, in East Sussex, the big woods and spreading sandy commons that are an attractive feature in the West Sussex landscape (explored in Route 11). There are lots of A roads, and even the B roads are too busy for enjoyable cycling – in fact it is hard to get among these pleasant flattish farmlands without having to contend with traffic. For example, the villages of Glynde and Firle, just east of Lewes, are frustratingly located off the lethally crowded A27. You will find it easy to vary or supplement the routes given for the High Weald, but Route 8, a circular tour of the Ouse valley beginning and ending at Lewes, is one of very few extended rides on lanes across this flatter country.

Behind Eastbourne, beyond where the South Downs plunge into the Channel at Beachy Head, lies East Sussex's one sizeable lowland district without major roads – Pevensey Levels, reclaimed land, where drainage ditches had been dug as early as the eighth century, so we learn from a charter of King Offa.

It was across the Levels that I rode on an extraordinarily warm February day in 1990 to return to the upland country around Brightling, Burwash and Mayfield. I make no apology for concentrating on the lanes of the High Weald in this chapter, for apart from its intrinsic beauty, already glimpsed in the Kentish routes (Chapter 6), this region has the attraction of being relatively little known. I have lived in East Sussex for most of the last twenty-five years, but only lately did I find my way among these broken hills, rolling prospects of wood and field, rural towns and steep valleys. Little seems to have changed since Edward A Martin wrote in the early 1930s that

> undoubtedly many more visit the Downs than they do the
> beautiful, though wild, Weald of Sussex, which to most people is
> a terra incognita. They pass through it by railway or coach, and
> comment on its beauty, but only they who walk through it, or
> even pass by a two-wheeler through some of its more unknown
> roads, really have any knowledge of what it has to offer.

Even today, when people travel by car rather than by
coach or train, these 'more unknown roads' are fairly
empty. They are good exercise, with their dips and climbs.
For the adventurous explorer by 'two-wheeler', they offer
some of the finest cycling in the south-east.

Place-names in the Weald often point towards its
character and history. Anywhere that ends in '-hurst' is a
reminder of the thick woods that once made all this area
impenetrable, and still today almost any Wealden view
includes generous stretches of copse or forest. Then there
are all those names reminiscent of the iron industry which
flourished as late as Napoleonic times: a glance at the OS
map reveals Ordnance Place (where artillery must have
been cast), Huggett's Furnace, Cinderhill Farm, Bivelham
Forge Farm, Ashburnham Forge, Furnace Cottage. . . . A
much-quoted passage from Camden's *Britannia* (1586)
describes the Wealden scene some decades after the
industry had been given a fresh impetus by the
introduction of the blast furnace:

> Full of iron it is in sundry places where for the making and fining
> whereof there be furnaces on every side and a huge deal of wood
> is yearly spent, to which purpose divers brooks in many places
> are brought to run in one channel and sundry meadows turned
> into pools and waters, that they might be of a power sufficient to
> drive hammer mills which beating upon the iron resound all over
> the places adjoining.

The line of these 'hammer ponds' can be traced right

across both East and West Sussex: the Ouse above Lewes
has its 'Iron River', north-east of Barcombe Mills, for
instance, and above Chithurst (near Trotton on the main
Petersfield to Midhurst road) 'Hammer Wood' and
'Hammer Stream' are marked.

Camden's words evoke an image almost pastoral in
today's terms: we are used to industry on a quite different
scale. The workings are long abandoned now, and no
hammers break the quiet of the 'brooks . . . meadows,
pools and waters'. You could very well lengthen out the
lovely two days' ride over by Burwash (Route 10), staying
an extra night there or at nearby Mayfield, by adding
some exploratory strolls or rides among relics of the
Wealden iron workings, put out of business when the
availability of coal for smelting, and of more robust water
power, moved the industry up to the new factory
landscapes of Coalbrookdale.

Iron made many family fortunes. Bateman's, Burwash,
where Rudyard Kipling lived and which stands in one of
the loveliest wooded valleys I know, was built for an
ironmaster in 1634. Up at airy, lofty Brightling (Route 9),
where you can gaze across wooded ridges running, as if
forever, away north into Kent, you will see a choice group
of follies ornamenting the parkland that once belonged to
'Mad Jack' Fuller, another landowner whose family made
their money in Wealden iron.

In East Sussex (as in Kent), you feel the closeness of
London, the pressure of population density and ever-
increasing car use. Finding these quiet routes required
some ingeniousness, even though I have been exploring
this county by bike for a decade now. Of course the
crowdedness of the landscape does have compensating
advantages: plenty of shops and pubs, abundant

accommodation. There is a reasonably good rail network, with the north–south routes from London to Hastings, Lewes, Uckfield and Brighton supplemented by the coastway line between Brighton and Hastings. Alas, you cannot simply get off at any station and ride into the countryside: careful route-planning is required, especially in summer. But if these descriptions inspire you to find your way onto East Sussex's quiet lanes, you will enjoy the reward of some fine riding.

Route 8:
The Sussex Ouse North of Lewes

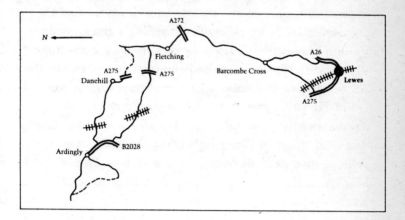

Lewes circular

South of Lewes, the Ouse is best left to walkers, who can get away from the unpleasantly busy roads and take footpaths along its embankments across the water-meadows. North of Lewes, however, the valley offers lovely cycling. It has plenty of variety: pastures, small fields of crops, woods and hedgerows and copses, and the Ouse itself with its murmuring tributaries. Through traffic keeps to the A roads to east and west, and although there will be cars on sunny summer weekends, this is some of the quietest cycling in mid-Sussex.

North of the A272, the scale of the landscape becomes less intimate, and the lanes feel slightly less rural: you will see that I followed paths and tracks to find deeper seclusion. But the going is still quiet and pleasant, if a little more strenuous, and popular Ardingly reservoir has plenty of space to accommodate summer visitors. Its shores are a good place to picnic before you turn and ride back south.

At forty-two miles, this is a moderately energetic day trip for a cyclist with some experience. Those who would rather take it easy can cut the distance down to about twenty-seven miles by riding from Ardingly reservoir on lanes into Haywards Heath, and picking up a train there (as Haywards Heath is on the Lewes line, you can use the same ticket back to London). Alternatively, the section north of Fletching can be left out altogether. This gives a delightful twenty-mile round trip from Lewes – with lunch, perhaps, in either of Fletching's two pubs, both of which have attractive gardens overlooking woods and fields.

Lewes circular

Distance: 42 miles. OS 198

Duration: Day trip (the route can be adapted as explained above, or its northern part omitted, to shorten the distance)

Terrain: Rolling, mostly quite gentle, but with some longer and steeper gradients, especially NW of Fletching. Here, low gears are required unless you are happy to get off and push. At one point, paths and tracks are followed. These will be difficult or impassable in wet conditions, and in any case you will have to lift your machine over two stiles. But an easy alternative on lanes is clearly indicated in the itinerary.

Itinerary: Trains to **Lewes** from London Victoria and from Brighton.
   Leave Lewes on the A275 (East Grinstead road), and turn off right at Offham church on lane to Hamsey and Barcombe, continuing NNE through Barcombe Cross to Spithurst church (grid ref. 425175). 1½ miles beyond Spithurst, fork right to cross the Ouse at Sharpsbridge and then via Piltdown Pond to the A272. Cross this and take the lane NW to **Fletching** (10 miles).

Continue N of Fletching through two lane crossroads to track which turns off left at grid ref. 429266. This is signposted to Wilmshurst and marked Private Road, with the Public Footpath marker beneath this notice. At the cottage, take the footpath through gate and across N edge of field to stile in NW corner. Climb this, follow the path down and then up (over another stile), and join the forestry track (grid ref. 424269). Navigate S and W through woods to find the lake (grid ref. 415258). Follow footpath and then track across foot of lake and to Furner's Green, taking the A275 NNW for less than 1 mile before forking off left to climb lane to Danehill church. After a few yards back on the main road, take lane left to Horsted Keynes village. (*Alternative route avoiding paths and tracks*: take left at Splayne's Green, at first lane crossroads N of Fletching, and continue on lanes just N of W to cross the A275 at grid ref. 411248. Continue N of W on lanes almost to Freshfield Halt station, but turn right on lane just before railway and so to Horsted Keynes village.) From Horsted Keynes, take lane NW to pass under railway just S of Horsted Keynes station, then ride W and turn left at grid ref. 359290, to join the B2028 for Ardingly village. Here double back SW on lane signposted 'Reservoir and College', turning back NW (grid ref. 339281) on signposted lane to **Ardingly Reservoir** (22 miles).

Walk along marked paths on E shore of reservoir to join lane (grid ref. 333298) leading back uphill to Ardingly village. Take the B2028 S as far as Stone Cross (grid ref. 358274). Here turn off left and navigate on lanes SE to Freshfield Halt (grid ref. 379256), and after passing beneath railway continue on lanes S of E to cross the A275 and so to Splayne's Green (grid ref. 431244) where you turn right to **Fletching** (31 miles).

Between Fletching and Barcombe Cross, follow outward route in reverse direction. At Barcombe Cross, take lane left to head SE and cross Ouse at Barcombe Mills (grid ref. 431149). Continue SE, turning off right on lane just before reaching the A26 and riding through Upper Wellingham before eventually reaching the A26 at grid ref. 428124 and so into **Lewes** (42 miles).

The simplest way from Lewes station to the East Grinstead road – pushing up Station Street and riding west along the High Street – will give you a glimpse of the castle, the most prominent of the town's historic buildings (though its dominance of the skyline has been usurped first by the nineteenth-century prison and more recently by the massive concrete County Hall). There is a well-displayed museum in the castle gate, and from the top of the keep you gain a panorama of the surrounding countryside. Looking north, you see the square tower of lonely Hamsey church, and behind it the Ouse valley, green and leafy in late spring and summer or patched with pale stubblefields and reddish ploughlands in autumn.

Despite the building of a bypass and tunnel in the 1970s, Lewes is much plagued by cars, and the A275 is a busy road. All the more pleasant is the contrast as you leave it, less than a mile out of town, to drop into the valley: you hear birdsong again, and smell the earth. The unassuming villages and gently sloping fields lack obvious drama, but their charm soon takes hold of you. Stopping just beyond St Bartholomew's at Spithurst, where the overgrown churchyard is set into a patch of woodland, I sat on a bank in autumn sunlight and thought how lucky I was to live so close to such pleasant country. This was late September, with a cool northerly breeze and misty grey-white clouds against the blue. Nature seemed fertile rather than melancholy. Ripe conkers and green acorns crunched underwheel in the lanes, and berries hung on the holly bushes. The leaves of the horse chestnuts were just turning at the crown of the trees, but the oaks still wore deep summer green. Some fields were stubble-covered, with fresh grass springing between the cornstalks; some were just ploughed; and in some, early-sown wheat was already an inch high and more.

All around Spithurst there are leafy lanes, with dappled shadows in sunny weather. The road dips and rises, crossing the Longford stream (where there is a good walk on a footpath along the south bank, with a view of imposing Newick Place) and then, at Sharpsbridge, the Ouse itself. Here there is a raised footway beside the road for use when floodwater rises. Crossing the busy east–west A272 at Piltdown Pond, a not very pastoral piece of water set amidst golf links and parked cars, you ride into more open country, with longer perspectives towards the narrow ridge of the South Downs west of Lewes.

Fletching has a single street, running past the church and between tall houses of weathered brick. The Griffin and the Rose and Crown are both nice pubs. The village remains unspoiled (it has no main road to contend with), but there is no feeling of over-preservation or artificial prettiness.

From Fletching to Ardingly you are skirting the edge of Ashdown Forest, a tract of heathland and mixed wood which merges, east towards Crowborough, into the more broken and greener hills of the lovely Sussex Weald (see Routes 9 and 10). I decided to follow footpaths and forestry tracks through Sheffield Forest. Only bridle paths, not footpaths, are officially open to cyclists. But if you give way readily and courteously to walkers, and take care not to harm crops or vegetation, no one is likely to take objection to your bike. You may have to hoist it over stiles, however, and you may find, as I did, that some paths are steep or narrow. If you have to keep to a tight timetable, if the weather is wet (or has recently been wet), or if you dislike the prospect of carrying your machine occasionally, then footpaths are best avoided (see in the itinerary, above, for an easy alternative on lanes). But paths and tracks do take you into some delightfully quiet places.

Alongside the grassy rides of Sheffield Forest, birch and

bracken do well in the sandy soil. Here and there the sandstone crops out in sizeable rocks. You will see it used as a building material locally, for instance in the churches at Danehill and Fletching.

It can be hard to keep one's bearings among these forestry tracks. Not all of them seem to be shown even on the 1:50 000 map, and woods are notoriously disorientating. You may think you will end up like the knight in the Victorian poem:

> The rider leant
> Forward to sound the marish with his lance.
> You saw the place was deadly; that doomed pair,
> The wretched rider and the hide-bound steed,
> Feared to advance, feared to return – That's all.
>
> (Lord de Tabley, *The Knight in the Wood*)

It was not quite that bad. I did get lost, but the sun, due south at 1300 hrs BST, directed me to the edge of the wood. I followed the margin of the trees, where a field sloped away towards Sheffield Green, and then doubled back under overhanging branches and half-walked, half-slithered – dragging my bike sometimes, and sometimes dragged along by it – down to the edge of the lake whose shining water was the landmark I had been looking for.

This lake was once a mill pond. The mill is long disused, and the stream flows out by a weir 'built' (so the inscription says) 'by S. Whitten, father and son' in 1964. I found it quite deserted. There were clear still reflections of the willows, pines, ash and other tall trees growing at the water's edge. Many traces remained of the havoc wrought all across Sussex by the great gale of October 1987 – an ill wind that brought some good, I suppose, since all along the ride I had been admiring piles of sawn firewood.

Sitting on a tree-trunk, I had some soup and some coffee: lunch for the 'wretched rider'; the 'hide-bound

steed' would have to make do with its morning's breakfast
of oil and air.

Ardingly reservoir, which you reach by lanes that run
beneath the line of the popular Bluebell Railway, is one of
several reservoirs constructed over the last twenty years in
this part of the world. Others are at Arlington, near
Eastbourne, and at Bewl Water and Darwell in the Weald.
Careful landscaping and well-managed access have made
them into local amenities: let us hope that they remain
open under the new privatised water regime.

Ardingly serves a dual function of reserve supply and
flow management. Although it was very low when I was
there, with a wide strip of sandy clay exposed all round its
shores, water was still being drawn off downstream,
presumably to keep up the level of the Ouse, on whose
tributary, the Shell river, the dam lies. There is a dinghy
sailing school, and fishing is provided for, as well as
canoeing and windsurfing.

Anglers, sheltered from the breeze under big green
umbrellas, and not catching much from the look of it,
dotted the banks while I finished my coffee on the grass.

My way back lay close to the way I had come out, and
indeed followed it exactly between Fletching and
Barcombe. But there is no sense of repetition: riding south,
the views are quite new. Turning off the B road at Stone
Cross, I found myself on a quiet lane, with the ridge of the
Downs away on the horizon, and open fields beside me
where pheasants scurried and squawked in the stubble.
Later, beyond Spithurst, dropping to the bridge over the
Bevern stream, the prospect towards Barcombe Cross
brings out the village's lovely setting on higher ground
above the Ouse. The river valley and the flat land north-

east of Lewes lie beyond, in pastoral calm.

I turned down to the riverside at Barcombe Mills. It was a while since I had been there. I was sorry to read, on a notice at the lane's end, of the closure of the quaint tearooms and boating establishment nearby: like Wemmick's house in *Great Expectations*, these always seemed to have been built of whatever materials lay to hand, in vain but obstinate imitation of some grander place. Our children, Jude and Maddy, in their younger days, took picnic parties of school friends there, for Kate and me to row them in flat-bottomed boats between the overgrown banks. Simple, perfect summer birthdays. . . .

The stretch of mown grass by the water was still accessible, and attractive, even though notices warned *Danger, Deep Water, No Swimming*. The river can hardly have got deeper since we used to bathe there, but it has certainly got less enticing. The long reach above the weir (which is the upper limit of the tidal flow) was covered with a bloom of scum. But, all in all, this was a good last pause on a lovely ride. Lifting my eyes from the water, I followed the line of trees upstream to where the river curves out of sight. It was too chilly for swimming anyhow, I reckoned. Too autumnal. Around me on the bank, someone had made small fires of cut twigs and scythed weeds, and their smoke rose mistily against the late afternoon sun.

Route 9:
The Weald and the Rother

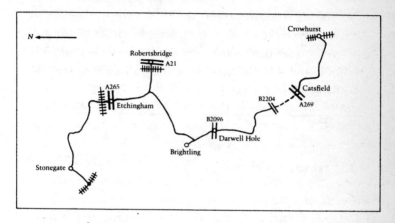

Crowhurst to Stonegate

The High Weald is the best cycling country in East Sussex. This day trip is a splendid introduction to it. The line of railway between Tunbridge Wells and Hastings crosses lovely country, and this route, after climbing up to Brightling, high on the Weald's south-eastern flank, drops into the Rother valley to switch back and forth across railway and river. To some extent, then, it falls into two parts: rolling and dipping hills, followed by valley terrain. Even after Robertsbridge, however, riding zig-zag north-west from station to station, you will find plenty of exercise as you climb out of the Rother meadows onto the higher, drier ridges that flank them and between which the tributary streams flow.

This is strenuous going: twenty-three miles of constant hills will provide most cyclists with exercise enough for a full day. If you have children with you, you may want to shorten the route – which is easily done, since you can pick up a train back to London from Robertsbridge or Etchingham if you decide not to push on as far as Stonegate.

Conversely, you can extend the ride, perhaps making it the basis of a weekend stay, by taking in either of the two celebrated attractions in the region, Battle Abbey and Bodiam Castle, both of which are within half a dozen miles of the route followed here.

Crowhurst to Stonegate

Distance: 23 miles. OS 199

Duration: Day trip (the route can easily be shortened as explained above)

Terrain: Strenuous, with many steep and some longish climbs. At one point a bridle path through woods is taken. In winter and spring, and after heavy rain at any season, this will be impassable: an alternative on lanes is given below.

Itinerary: Trains to **Crowhurst** (on the Hastings line) from London Charing Cross and London Bridge.

Ride S from Crowhurst station. Turn left opposite the church and then fork right (grid ref. 757118) to climb steeply onto the lane running just N of W to Henley's Down. Fork right to Catsfield, taking lane left of the church and crossing the main A269 road. Take the marked bridle path NW through the woods to Steven's Crouch (grid ref. 711154). (*Alternative route avoiding bridle path*: At Catsfield, ride a few score yards left down A269 and take lane on right. Follow this to junction at grid ref. 708134, where take right and so up to the B2204 and Steven's Crouch.) At Steven's Crouch cross the B2204 and take lanes NW to Darwell Hole on the B2096. Cross that road and continue on lanes to **Brightling** (grid ref. 684210) (9 miles).

From Brightling ride NE via Oxley's Green to lane junction at grid ref. 719235. If you wish to visit the town, ride E to **Robertsbridge** (13 miles).

Riding back out to the lane junction, this time take the right fork and ride just W of N to Etchingham. Take the A265 right for a couple of hundred yards before taking the lane left, then left again at T-junction to ride along the ridge to Stonegate (grid ref. 668285). From Stonegate village drop on the lane past the church down to **Stonegate station** (23 miles).

Trains run from Stonegate station to London Charing Cross and London Bridge.

Looking back on this ride the day after making it, I recall the spring-like warmth and calm we enjoyed. The late October leaves were turning, and many of them had been stripped from the trees by gales the week before, so there were reminders of autumn in every view and every roadside hedge or copse. The earth was damp from night fogs, and autumn smells were heavy: despite the green of the pastures, brought back to vigorous growth after a parching summer, there was no mistaking the season. A milky autumnal haze blurred the characteristic Wealden views, with ridges rising one above the next into the blue distance. But it was warm enough to ride in a T-shirt, to sit on a sylvan bench lazily drinking coffee, to lunch in the pub garden of the Seven Stars in Robertsbridge. When I remarked on the lovely weather to the proprietress of the Stores in Stonegate, she replied that we were making the most of it – myself and my son Jude, who at twelve years old was already causing me to wonder when he will outstrip me on the hill climbs. Making the most of it: indeed we were.

Today, as I write, another westerly gale full of driving rain is lashing the bent trees. That golden calm seems a whole season ago. And there is the same lost, irrecoverable quality in the landscape of the High Weald: it is hard to believe, once out of it and back into more frequented country, that the arc of silent farmland and forest which runs for a dozen miles south-east from Mayfield is not a dream.

Crowhurst is almost as quiet a station as you will find in Sussex. The parked cars in the yard – here and at the other stations you pass later – show plainly enough that this is commuting country: the railway is for business first, pleasure second. But Crowhurst, linked though it is to the City, feels deeply rural. It is well endowed with trees and hedges, true to the 'hurst' in its name. Crowhurst, Wadhurst, Lamberhurst, Ticehurst, Goudhurst: this is among the commonest place-name elements hereabouts. Riding – or pushing – up out of Crowhurst onto the ridge that runs north-west, you will enjoy views of woodland across intervening pasture fields on both sides of the road. From time to time, when woods are more to the foreground and you see clearly the border where farmed fields meet scrubby undergrowth (always ready to spread back onto untended pasture), you get a sense of how, with much labour over many centuries, this whole region was won from the primeval forest.

Most if not all of the extensive plantations to be seen nowadays are recent rather than ancient, however. Beyond Catsfield, Jude and I pushed our bikes up through mixed woodland: birch, conifers, coppiced chestnut. This last is a long-standing feature, for coppiced woods fed the furnaces of Sussex's ironworks from Roman times until the late eighteenth century.

Entering the wood, we passed anglers dozing by a pond, one of them wrapped in a sleeping bag and sprawled on a deckchair. Feeling lazy ourselves, we stopped for coffee on a curiously deep bench-like structure, which bore the number 10 on a large blue label and was marked by a triangular wooden flag. Jude had his theory about this: the bench had been built by Cubs, he decided, in some competition, and 10 was the number of the Cub pack. . . . But no: I discovered a notice pinned to the slats. This was a piece of horse apparatus, 'a dressing-fence in the pairs'.

We had passed several riders, and the wood was full of signposts intended for customers of the riding school back by the main road. Horses and bicycles, alas, are not altogether compatible on woodland paths (or across fields, either): hooves soon churn wet surfaces into a sticky morass, which four legs can still just about get through but where two wheels are worse than useless.

Wherever it dipped into a hollow, the sandy clay of the track grew black and glutinous. The Wealden clay is notoriously stiff: John Talbot White (in *The South-East Down and Weald*) says of the old turn-wrist plough, with its massive three-yard-long oak beam, that 'its very weight enabled it to work the heavy clays of the Weald. . . . Without it, the Weald could not have been won.' Jude and I had more trouble with sticky mud at the end of our ride. As for this track, it is best avoided in wet conditions. But on a dry summer or autumn day, take it, for it will bring you right in among trees and bracken-grown clearings, into the scents and sounds of the woods.

Back on surfaced lanes north of the B2204, we swooped down past a curious hexagonal tower into a stream valley. Then came the climb back out. I love these swoops and climbs, though they are hard work. From here towards

Brightling, in every sense the high point of this route, the climbing is fairly steady. You have leisure to admire the views and the many old roadside houses, with their warm brick, painted weather-boarding or decorative half-tiling.

As you climb into Brightling village, you will see on the left the slate rooves of the manor house. Brightling Park, landscaped (it is thought) by Capability Brown, has a collection of early nineteenth-century follies. These, and the village church, are the sights of Brightling. St Thomas à Becket's church is built in the local sandstone of the Hastings Beds, a stone that finds and reflects warm lights in the sunshine all year round. Its fabric dates mainly from the thirteenth and fourteenth centuries, and the interior has many interesting memorials and monuments, including some early brasses. With its short, almost stumpy tower, the building is homely rather than elegant. The churchyard – solidly walled where it borders Brightling Park, and cropped when we were there by a local farmer's sheep – makes a fine setting. As you walk back down the brick pathway to the gate, the green land over to Kent lies open to the eye, and the top of the Weald feels like the top of the world: there are few higher points, and perhaps no higher village, in East Sussex.

This elevated situation recently attracted the attention of the electronics firm Racal, who decided, and gained planning permission, to build a large radio aerial on the skyline nearby: nominally this is for the benefit of car-phone users, but protesting posters all over the village suggest that it will really form part of something called 'Hi-Fix 6', a new anti-missile defence system. Angry letters to the local MP had achieved nothing, the owner of the village shop told us: the concrete base of the aerial was already being laid.

This modern folly will not lack companions, at any rate.

The follies of 'Mad Jack' Fuller have attracted many tales – that he was buried in top hat and dinner dress, claret glass in hand, in the pyramidal mausoleum you will hardly fail to notice in the churchyard; that the observatory built by the Brightling–Burwash road was for the convenience of his servants, so they could keep watch for his coach returning from the House of Commons; that the so-called Sugar Loaf, a conical building near Woods Corner on the highway from Heathfield to Battle, was erected because Fuller had wagered he could see Dallington church spire from his estate: when he found he could not, he is said to have had the Sugar Loaf, which looks remarkably like the spire, put up overnight so he could win his bet.

John Fuller (1757–1834) was hardly the genial philanthropic squire whom local tradition would like to celebrate (his life and times are related in a pamphlet by Geoff Hutchinson on sale in the church). The family fortune, made in Wealden iron workings, was invested in West Indian plantations, and as an MP Fuller was a staunch defender of slavery and the slave trade. He won the contested East Sussex seat by playing on local anti-Catholic feeling. Perhaps Fuller's patronage of J M W Turner, who several times visited the estate to make drawings and engravings, and his various local good works can be put in the balance against all this?

At all events, the tour from one folly to the next, all set among fields and woods on the top of the Weald, would make a delightful two hours' summer stroll or ride. The booklet I mention, by Geoff Hutchinson, together with the OS map, will guide you on your way. One folly, the Gothic tower set among a beech plantation (much damaged in the 1987 storm), is visible as you ride up into the village from Darwell Hole.

★

After Brightling it is an easy run down to Robertsbridge. The fine High Street (once pounded mercilessly by traffic on the A2100, a bypass has now opened) is the core of the town: a Victorian United Reformed Church Hall blends surprisingly well with a range of older buildings. Out towards the open country there are inter-war and post-war houses and estates, and several imposing red-brick villas which must date from the opening of the railway. Back in town, on the flat land by the Glottenham stream, and also on the lane west, we saw the concrete foundations being poured over the land for two new developments.

The rural lane to Etchingham dips and climbs: ridge, valley, ridge, valley, ridge, valley. It is beautiful, but Jude said his legs ached. At Etchingham you have the first moment of real flatness, among the serene water-meadows of the Dudwell and the Rother. Now the riding gets easier, for you follow a long ridge to Stonegate town, with hills to the south and the line of a Wealden road to the north, where solid-looking Ticehurst church is the most conspicuous building. Then you drop back to river and railway. There is plenty of scope to walk or picnic while you wait for the evening train (they come at least once an hour). Paths run along the north bank of the Rother: Jude and I foolishly took our bikes with us when we explored them, and regretted it when the wheels were caked with mud in minutes. Or you can ride a little way west on quiet lanes and brew tea by one of the bridges near Bivelham Farm, with river flats all round and woodland and hedges in the middle distance and the ridges of the Weald framing the sky above.

Route 10:
Pevensey Levels, Burwash, Ashdown Forest

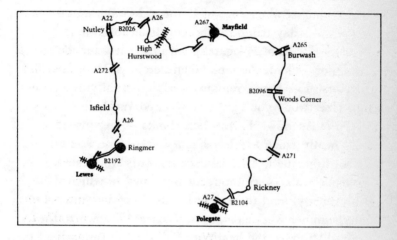

Polegate to Lewes

Always, it seems, I have been more than fortunate with the weather when I have cycled in the Weald – most spectacularly on this trip, when two glorious blue days were sandwiched between savage rainy gales. The Weald is the heart of this ride. From Herstmonceux over to High Hurstwood, the elements of the landscape remain constant: stream valleys, fields of pasture and tillage running among patches of tangled wood, steep hills, fine prospects from the ridges over miles of rolling land. Even under less favourable skies, this is country to soothe and enchant the eye.

Despite the pounding of traffic on the A roads (a bypass is planned for Mayfield), Burwash and Mayfield are small, homely towns. In the evening they grow quiet, and smell

of woodsmoke. Either makes a pleasant overnight stay.
You can wander from pub to pub beneath the
unpretentious vernacular housefronts, tile-hung or
weather-boarded.

You ride towards the Weald across Pevensey Levels, a
smaller-scale reminiscence of Romney Marsh, and a very
easy run. (A day trip onto the Levels, a dozen miles'
circular route from Polegate, is an ideal introduction to
cycling for a child: the lane taken here, by Down Level
and Horse Eye Level, remains fairly quiet all year.) After
High Hurstwood you leave the wooded Weald and cross
the top of Ashdown Forest, hereabouts an expanse of
sandy heath which actually has few trees, and is quite
distinct from the nearby landscapes. It is worth seeing, but
it is really walkers' country, for the lanes, of which there
are not many, tend to be a little busy even in winter. On
sunny summer weekends I would leave Ashdown to the
cars and trippers: the heath, and all the roads over and to
it, get crowded. (The route can easily be shortened to cut
out the last stretch: Jarvis Brook station, with trains to
London via Tunbridge Wells, is only a few miles north-
east of Mayfield along pleasant lanes.)

After Nutley, heading back south to Lewes, you are
skirting the eastern Ouse valley (so that this ride
complements Route 8, which runs to the west of the river).
The scenery is less dramatic than in the Weald, but there
are similar views over fields, woods and streams. Here the
going is almost all downhill or on the level, a welcome
respite at the end of a strenuous trip: between
Herstmonceux and High Hurstwood, and especially after
Burwash, you must put in plenty of hard climbing to pay
for the lovely views and swooping descents. To enjoy
cycling here you must be reasonably fit – or else be happy
to take things slowly (why not?), getting off to push on the

hills, and perhaps cutting short the second day by picking up a train at Jarvis Brook.

Polegate to Lewes

Distance: 58 miles. OS 199, 198

Duration: Two days (one short day, one long day)

Terrain: Flat before Herstmonceux and after Nutley, but hilly and demanding in the central section. At Herstmonceux Castle the route follows a bridle path which is difficult or impassable when wet: an alternative route on lanes and a short stretch of A road is given.

Itinerary: Trains to **Polegate** from London Victoria.

Leaving Polegate station, head N to join the Hastings road (A27) at about 300 yards, and there turn right. After just over half a mile turn left down Levett Road, which takes you through the housing estate and then heads NE to cross the B2104 at grid ref. 604062. Turn right and then left at T-junctions to reach Rickney. Here turn E but just past farm buildings turn right to head N across the Levels via New Bridge to lane junction at grid ref. 627113, turning right via Golden Cross and Cherry Croft Farm to **Herstmonceux church** (9 miles).

Follow the bridleway (marked 'Bridleway to Wartling') below the castle and back up to the lane which runs N to join the A271 a little E of Windmill Hill. (*Alternative route avoiding bridle path*: Back at Golden Cross, take lanes N to A271, and then turn right.) Turn right off the main road at grid ref. 656119. Follow lanes keeping where possible to the most northerly route, so via Brownings Farm, Bray's Hill, Brownbread Street, Pont's Green and Herrings Farm to **Wood's Corner** (17 miles).

From Wood's Corner follow the lane that runs just E of N to **Burwash** (21 miles). (To visit Bateman's and the Dudwell valley, detour left of this lane just before it climbs into Burwash village.)

From Burwash, take the lane that leaves the A265 NW at grid ref. 670245. Follow this round to the T-junction at grid ref. 645245. Turn right, then left, past Great Bines and across the Rother and so bearing left to Bivelham Farm (grid ref. 631264). Continue W on this lane until you reach the T-junction at grid ref. 603263, where you turn right and bear round into **Mayfield** (28 miles).

Leave Mayfield by the last of three lanes right off the A267, by the Railway Arms pub, following this lane back to the main road at Butcher's Cross (grid ref. 560255). Keep on lanes WSW via Pigsfoot Farm to the lane crossroads by Stockland Farm and at the crossroads at grid ref. 525247, turn right to ride NNW over the railway line to Burnt Oak (grid ref. 514270). Ride W and then S to High Hurstwood, where you turn back N and follow the lane up to the A26 at **Poundgate** (grid ref. 494288) (38 miles).

Turn left and follow the main road for less than 1 mile, taking the lane right signposted to Duddleswell and Nutley, crossing the B2026 and over Ashdown Forest to the A22, where you turn left into **Nutley** (43 miles).

Turn right off the main road as you leave Nutley (at grid ref. 443275). Follow this lane as it runs almost due S to cross the A272 near Piltdown, and continue S via Isfield to the A26 at grid ref. 450156. Here take the main road S for a couple of hundred yards before turning off left on the public bridleway (this is a farm track with a firm rubble surface passable even in wet weather). Go through the farm buildings and follow the track E (the marked right of way is just S of the track but the farmer is happy to let walkers and cyclists use the track). When you reach the lane (grid ref. 460143), turn right and follow the lane to Ringmer and the B2192, which you take, turning right and riding SW via a short stretch of the A26 into **Lewes** (58 miles).

Trains run from Lewes to London Victoria.

Clear of close-knit, suburban Polegate, you drop out of the housing estate to cross farmland before reaching the Levels. Here, the changing seasons leave rather little mark on the landscape. No ploughland, few trees: green is everywhere, and already in late February the new grass was springing. But the thorn hedges were wintry still: in May and June, their white and pink blossom makes a fine sight.

Beside the lanes, full drainage channels lay blue, gently

ruffled. The sky and the southerly breeze would have graced April. On this I agreed with the cyclist who overtook me between Horse Eye and New Bridge: his green jersey, emblazoned in white with *Lewes Wanderers Cycling Club*, bobbed in the lane ahead until he pulled out of sight. At the bridge, I stopped to drink coffee from my flask, sitting on my cape in moist grass – and stinging my wrists on the new season's tiny, venomous nettles.

The drainage had risen to the challenge of the previous month's heavy rains. A few days earlier, crossing West Sussex by train, I had seen extensive floods in the Arun valley, but here above Pevensey there were no more than a few pools and marshy patches. Riding on, I saw a heron by one rushy puddle. It turned its head stiffly to watch me pass, but did not take wing – with that heavy wingbeat, clumsy when you see and hear it close by, measured and graceful at a distance.

Herstmonceux was, until recently, the site of the Greenwich Observatory (Greenwich air having become too smoggy long ago). It was from here that the time-keeping pips were relayed to the BBC. I am not sure what is to become of the site now: I did not ask, as the answer is probably depressing: some exclusive conference centre or health farm. Mind you, the Observatory always made you feel fairly excluded, too, with tough-looking fences and warning notices.

Even under new ownership, the bridle path will presumably remain a right of way, taking you just below the smooth-lawned, brick-built castle. Here you have fine views back south over the Levels. This is a good introduction, too, to the famous Wealden clay – 'good', in the sense of savage and uncompromising. Foolishly, eyeing the horse-churned morass but not wanting to double back and be forced onto the main road (however briefly), I shouldered my bike and plunged in. Soon enough I was 'in . . . so far / Returning were as tedious as go o'er': within a few yards of the mud starting, it was up to my calves. My socks and shoes got wet, grey, glutinous. . . . Stopping at the disused car park where the path rejoins lanes, cleaning the worst of the mud off the tyres (and also, alas, changing a punctured tube), I watched a boy and his dad play with their remote control model car. Round and round it buzzed. Across the tarmac, back, across, back. Surely that kind of fun soon palls? – or is it just that I would find it dull from the start. More fun, more morally adventurous, I reflected, to plunge up to your knees in clay and, muddy but self-righteous, I got back onto my bike. Soon, I hoped, I would find clean water to wash my shoes and socks. (A few miles on, I did stop at a clear gravelly drainage channel beside a lane.) The landlord of the Bell Inn at Burwash, where my room was booked for the night, would not want me in his corridors in my present state.

After Herstmonceux you are off the Levels and rising, quite gradually, to the southern ridge of the Weald. Near Brightling (see also Route 9), you are on a fine high plateau. Although there is nowhere that offers a full 360-degree panorama, there are many wonderful views: from by the obelisk, which you pass (and which is much used as a surveyors' landmark), or if you detour a little, as I did, from all along below the crumbling stone wall that edges Brightling Park to the north.

It was early afternoon, and I had time to spare. Pushing my bike, strolling and pausing, breathing the pure air (it certainly tasted and felt pure), I wandered about the quiet upland lanes until I found the picnic site I had specified to myself: somewhere in the sun, sheltered from the breeze, dry underfoot and with a view.

You swoop down towards Burwash, a long freewheel through tree-hung lanes. In May 1989, Kate and I had passed this way on burning hot Cup Final Saturday, and had stopped to make tea in a corner of a field. Cup Final or no Cup Final, they were holding a big equestrian event up at Brightling Park, and the loudspeaker commentary floated and boomed in the thick heat of the valleys below. Horses and riders, ploughing matches and point-to-points, roast beef sandwiches in beery pubs, commuting to the City from Etchingham and Stonegate and Crowhurst: comfortable Toryism, faintly tinged with green – a long way from Anfield and Goodison and Wembley and Hillsborough. . . . But here, in the remote quiet of the Weald, is one of Britain's most important gypsum mining areas. There is a mine entrance on your right as you ride downhill, and an aerial ropeway, running for two or three miles above dense woods, links this to another and larger mine near Netherfield. Apart from the ropeway (which in its silent movement scarcely intrudes on the quiet valleys), neither the mine nor the associated plasterboard works makes much visible impact on the landscape.

Before entering Burwash village, I wandered in the low-lying pastoral water-meadows of the Dudwell, which separate the town up on its ridge from the wooded slopes that face it to the south. Bateman's, once Rudyard Kipling's home and now a National Trust property, stands at the edge of the river-flats, amidst rich grazing. The narrow Dudwell, fast flowing and creamy green when I was there, threads its way beneath a lane that runs up to the woods. Past the farm at the foot of the plantation (it has a listed camping site), up through a field where two caravans stood parked, I found my way in among the trees. Gale damage was extensive and very evident here, as it had been at several points during my morning ride. Stumbling and struggling among fallen trunks, I soon gave up my attempt to climb into the heart of the wood; instead I took it easy, sitting to drink tea at the plantation's edge, looking out through a screen of twigs at the grassy slopes.

Then, in the last warm sun, I went back down, took my bike from where I'd left it propped against a tree, and – pausing again to watch the water rush beneath the little bridge – walked back by the big house.

By Bateman's, Burwash, 4.00pm, 22 February 1990

Sitting on the brick platform in front of a wooden gazebo (?) – open to the public and dedicated 'In Memoriam Elsie Bambridge, 1896–1976'. The late afternoon sun still feels warm on the back of my hand as I write. The whole still, sheltered valley is drenched in its yellow light, and in birdsong.

Today does feel like the first day of spring. Signs of the new season: the sharp sting of young nettles as I sat to drink coffee on the Levels; the catkins I noticed hanging from the hazels in the hedges along this lane; the fact that all the cows seem let out, so the grass must be springing; the haze, purplish, faint but insistent, of the young birches' new shoots and formed, closed buds against the greyish background of still wintry woods below the ridge at Brightling. Alongside thriving, delicate snowdrops, there are daffodils in the verges, and also many primroses blooming – a dozen plants glimmering among dead leaves and withered grass on the slope to my right here. . . . Also, prosaically, at Bateman's the gardener was earlier buzzing up and down with his petrol mower, surely for the first time this year. . . . And poetically: among the chattering small birds and the caw of rooks, I hear now and have heard all the last hour, as I wandered across the bridge and in the forest, the gurgling, wood-lost call of pigeons, that rich cooing (almost gravelly) which I used, as a child, to mistake for unpractised cuckoos, and which will be heard now all spring and summer. Even today, when I can see on the slope across the river how bare the trees are, that call makes me think of the thick leaves and long sunlit evenings of May and June.

At the Bell Inn, Burwash, I spent a comfortable night. Eating in the bar before going early to bed, I noted that the collection of barometers, twenty or more of them, were all pointing to Set Fair. But maybe, ranged as they were above the glowing log fire, they would have said that even if it had been pouring down outside?

The first, hilly part of the next day's ride is still very much in Wealden woods, with oasthouses and a small hop garden lending a Kentish touch to the landscape. A lovely counterpart to the Dudwell valley is the valley of the Rother north of Burwash, where I stopped and sat awhile on the parapet of the bridge between Great Bines and Bivelham Farm. Then on, labouring happily across the slopes, through Mayfield (where I shopped) and across the Uckfield railway line to High Hurstwood. You must take circuitous routes to avoid the ridge roads, which are busy: the lanes are both scenic and almost carless.

Then, at Poundgate, comes the shock of traffic on the A26: you stay on the main road only for a few hundred yards, but it marks the end of the lost, secluded hills. As I have said, the lanes across Ashdown Forest, which you now reach, are less peaceful. The vegetation is distinctive: heather, pine and birch, and bracken – dead bracken, at this season, brown and crumpled. But this area, with its fenced-off military radio installations and its marked picnic sites every 500 yards beside the lanes and its three A class north–south major roads within five miles, is hardly the wilderness that Cobbett found so grim in January 1822:

Ashurst [i.e. Ashdown] Forest, which is a heath . . . verily the most villainously ugly spot I ever saw in England. This lasts you for four or five miles, getting, if possible, uglier and uglier all the way, till, at last, as if barren soil, nasty spewy gravel, heath and even that stunted were not enough, you see some rising spots, which instead of trees, present you with black, ragged, hideous rocks. There may be Englishmen who wish to see the coast of *Nova Scotia*. They need not go to sea; for here it is to the life.

Cobbett exaggerates for effect, of course (incidentally, his 'hideous rocks' must be the sandstone outcrop towards Tunbridge Wells, popular nowadays with mountaineers seeking practice in the generally unrugged Home Counties). He also sets himself squarely against the Romantic vogue for the barren and the wild: no unproductive heath, in his eyes, can compare with a nicely tended farmland. On this ride, you may well feel tempted to agree, for the luscious-looking stream valleys of the Weald are quite as beguiling as Ashdown (though the Wealden soils are not in fact particularly rich, and have always required careful husbandry). But then, as we have said, Ashdown Forest is not much of a wilderness nowadays. However, it has a pleasantly open and breezy feel, and long wide views away towards the Downs, to reflect the fact that you are some 600 feet above sea level before you leave the heath and drop towards Nutley.

My last stop, for a last cup of tea, was almost at the finish of the easy run to Lewes which ends this trip. I sat beside the farm track (open as a public bridleway) by Plashett Park Farm:

3.00pm, 23 February 1990

My view from here is an epitome of the inland scenery of these two days: green fields (all pasture, just here), with wintry thorn hedges running between them, and abutting on patchy copses where the white birch-trunks stand out in the sunlight. The land is less abrupt here than in the Weald, but it dips and rolls: down to a ditch or stream 300 yards in front of me, where the hedge is stragglier, with a willow or two among the unkempt thorns (and where a pig is rooting happily in the open among trodden mud); and then gently up to a line of woods. . . .

8. West Sussex

The elements of the East Sussex landscape – sea coast, Downs, and then an intervening plain before you come to the Weald – continue west over the county boundary. Within this continuity, however, there is a good deal that changes. Indeed, each half of Sussex is a distinctive region. Nothing in the West quite parallels the remoteness of parts of the Weald in north-east East Sussex, the green, airy situation of Brightling or Mayfield. Nothing in the East quite parallels the greensand hills of north-west West Sussex, with their bracken-grown woods and commons and the spacious, lost lowland villages (Lurgashall, Ebernoe) away behind them (Route 12).

The coast is as inhospitable to the cyclist here as it is further east. Since there are no cliffs to keep you away from the very edge of the sea, development has been even more continuous: in 1977 John Talbot White noted (in *The South-East Down and Weald*) that of the forty-three kilometres between Peacehaven and Bognor – a stretch lying mostly in West Sussex – only three kilometres were undeveloped: everywhere else, buildings line the shore. Beyond Bognor, there is small change. However, the Witterings and East Head, at the eastern mouth of Chichester harbour (not far from the Hampshire boundary), are good sandy beaches, with interesting tidal pools – if you can face braving summer traffic to get there. . . . At quieter times, a ride over the lanes of this flat land west of Bognor, the Manhood Peninsula as it is called, would probably provide as rural a seaside tour as you can find (Romney Marsh and Pevensey Levels apart) between Harwich and Southampton. But it would only last an hour or so, and you would see plenty of unplanned, unbeautiful building.

The routes given here stay inland. Both begin on the Downs, which swell, west of the Arun, to a broad ridge seven or eight miles across, a more complex and generous landscape than the bare narrow fin of chalk found further east. This is rolling, wooded country, with the cornfields that have largely replaced the old sheep-grazing set among beech and conifer afforestation. The sheep-cropped, wildflower-scented, thyme-flavoured turf which once made Southdown sheep and Southdown mutton so famous has all but disappeared. Parts of Sussex were arable before the Romans came, and more went under the plough during the Napoleonic wars, but the great expansion of corn-growing came in the Second World War. The grainfields are less rich in wildlife and make a less distinctively Sussex landscape than the grazing. No one will deny, however, that when the crop ripens and its golden ears and stalks billow in the wind, it makes a beautiful sight against dark green trees.

From the Arun valley westwards to the main A3 Portsmouth road (just into Hampshire) is some twenty miles as the crow flies. A couple of biggish roads cross the ridge, and some smaller ones too, but the whole area is wonderfully peaceful by contrast with the coastal plain to its south. It offers long pastoral walks and cycle rides, with fine views both south and north. East towards Arundel the tops carry no lanes, but there are bridle paths passable in reasonable weather, including the South Downs Way and Stane Street, the old Roman road from Chichester which we take near the start of Route 11. Further west, there are lanes as well as tracks, and even in high summer some of these are as peaceful as they are scenic. The ride west through the flint villages of East Dean and Singleton, and then the drop down through woods to Buriton just into Hampshire (Route 12), must be twenty of the finest miles of cycling in southern England.

There is fine riding north of the Downs too. Here again, however, the country is more attractive west of the 'Arun, if only because traffic density between Brighton and the Arun valley has grown steadily. Already in 1936 H J Massingham (in *English Downland*) was noting how 'the exquisite line of villages below the northern scarp between Amberley and Edburton – Storrington, Washington, Steyning, Bramber and Upper Beeding – are slowly surrendering their personal identity to the main road along which they are strewn.' The settlements are beginning to defend themselves at last: Bramber has its bypass and any motorist who chooses to enter the village is slowed by chicanes to a sensible seven or eight miles an hour. But the road, which as a teenager I remember cycling with pleasure, is not tolerable now.

West of Amberley, the villages and little towns are unspoiled and lie on the quietest of lanes. Bury, Bignor, Sutton, Graffham, Heyshott, Cocking, Bepton, Didling, Treyford, Elsted, Harting: for me, that is a powerful litany of place-names, carrying associations of a lovely piece of country – heaths, pinewoods, rhododendrons, sheep fields and horse pastures at the foot of the sudden, wooded scarp – and of my childhood's happiest days, the holidays and weekends we spent at my grandmother's in Sutton just south of Petworth.

Route 11, dropping from the top of Bignor Hill and looping west and east over the scarp foot, crosses this country and passes through these villages (with their simple, ancient churches) before taking you to the little station at Amberley.

Route 12 runs more quickly over this flatter land and over the Rother (which has the same name, oddly, as the main eastward-flowing river in East Sussex), into the greensand country mentioned above: some sharp climbs, some long climbs (the haul up to Bexley Hill . . .), quiet lanes and bridleways, ending with a remote, silent crossing of the Arun by footbridge.

As well as being beautiful, this landscape is notably rural in feel. There are some brilliant pubs: the Three Moles at Selham (Route 11) is a favourite of mine. Villages such as Graffham and South Harting still have real Village Stores, and in larger places just off-route (Midhurst, Petworth) you will find a Cream Tea if that is what you want.

Should you want to linger on your way, there are several places to visit. Some of these are mentioned in the route texts: Route 11 has Bignor Roman Villa and the churches at Didling and Elsted and Selham: Route 12 has Goodwood House, the open air Museum of Weald and Downland Life at Singleton, and Petworth House and Park. Also near Route 12 is Uppark, by Compton, recently burned out, but a full restoration is planned; and the route ends at Amberley station, where there is the Chalk Pits museum, with rural and Victorian industrial technology on display.

Accommodation is abundant. There are bed and breakfast places even in the less populous downland and scarp foot regions, for South Downs Way walkers provide steady custom. Several Guides to the South Downs Way exist (one is listed in the Booklist), and these contain addresses and phone numbers of suitable accommodation.

Book ahead in summer.

Is it possible to link East and West Sussex, riding across from Lewes (Routes 8 and 10)? You would have to cross the Adur and the Arun, and roads over these rivers are relatively few and correspondingly busy. If you look closely at the OS maps, however, you will see occasional bridleway crossings, and lanes bridge the rivers upstream. You would have to weave a rather circuitous course, well to the north of the busy through-ways below the Downs, but it could be done.

West Sussex is served by the Arun Valley railway from London, which takes you to Pulborough and Amberley (Routes 12 and 11). The coastway line west from Brighton via Chichester runs along the flat land by the sea. Both the routes given here start on this more southerly line and work back inland, north-east, to take advantage of the prevailing south-west winds.

Route 11:
Across and Below the West Sussex Downs

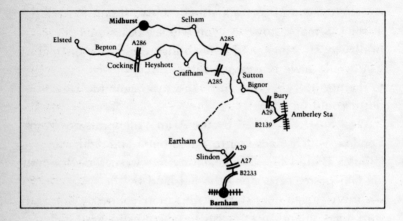

Barnham to Amberley

This ride explores an area which I revisit every year. It is almost my home – the 'home' of my most vivid childhood memories. My grandmother lived at Sutton, just south of Petworth, and we spent many weekends and, always, long summer weeks there. From the upstairs window where I lay and read, and convalesced after chicken pox, you could see the Downs west of Bignor Hill, their crest marked by two pylons. A score of walks led from the garden gate up through woods onto those open heights.

This route begins with a brief ride and a leisurely three-mile walk through woods and past cornfields up to the National Trust downland above Bignor. The South Downs Way runs past here, and this stretch, between Amberley and Harting Down, is of great variety and charm: woods, open country, prehistoric tumuli, long views north to the Weald and south to the Channel. Mountain bikers – we had a memorable encounter with one in the small hours – have not been slow to lay claim to these tracks: their speed and, too often, their seeming indifference to pedestrians can make them an intrusive presence. I always prefer to get off and push on rough tracks, taking things at the easier pace which this scenery deserves. However, all the tracks in this route are bridleways, so you are legally entitled to cycle them if you prefer.

The northern scarp of the Downs drops sharply. Between its foot and the main Petersfield–Petworth road lies a tract of sandy, quiet country, easy going along shady lanes, among heathy woods and giant rhododendrons. Selham, Elsted and Didling have interesting churches, worth visiting in their own right, and doubly worth visiting because to reach them you must cross this backwater – only a few miles from the main roads to and from the coast, but belonging, it seems, to a different world from those arteries of thundering holiday traffic.

This is too much riding (and walking) for a single day – who would want to rush it, anyway? – but it makes a leisurely two days' trip. Petworth, Midhurst, and several of the villages along the foot of the Downs have inns and bed and breakfasts. In summer, book ahead. Unfortunately there seem to be few official campsites. There used to be one at Coldharbour Farm, a great resource, a simple field with a water tap and views along what must be one of the loveliest valleys in Sussex. Now the farm has changed hands and is devoted to horse training and horse exercising. No more space for campers. Ask a farmer, or try putting up a tent by one of the downland tracks – but not in the rightly preserved triangle of National Trust land just west of Bignor Hill, where the prohibition against tents is strictly enforced.

Barnham to Amberley

Distance: approx. 46 miles. OS 197

Duration: Two days (one overnight stay)

Terrain: Mostly easy, but there is a steep descent on the scarp of the Downs, and the track up onto them (Stane Street), though well surfaced, is not metalled and would present problems after prolonged rain.

Itinerary: Trains run to **Barnham** from London Victoria (Bognor Regis line) and from Brighton and Portsmouth.

Leave Barnham station on the N side and take the road fronting the exit right as far as the first fork. Here (grid ref. 962045) fork left, and so via Walberton and across both the A27 and the A29 to Slindon (grid ref. 964084). Leave Slindon westwards, riding W and then NW to **Eartham** (grid ref. 939094) (5 miles).

Ride N out of Eartham until you enter Eartham Wood. Here find the path marked Stane Street, and follow this due NE until you reach the signpost and car park at grid ref. 973129. From here follow the steeply hollowed chalk track down via Coldharbour Farm (grid ref. 973136) to the lane junction at grid ref. 972148. (*Alternative route avoiding this steep descent*: from the signpost on the top of the Downs, take the metalled lane, itself quite steep, down to Bignor, grid ref. 983144. Then ride via S end of Sutton, grid ref. 979152, and SW to grid ref. 972148.) Now follow lane N to Barlavington and then W to meet the A285 at grid ref. 960163. Follow this main road N for 100 yards before turning off left on metalled lane, which later becomes a public byway (still metalled), through Seaford College and East Lavington to Graffham church (grid ref. 929166) and so N to **Graffham** (15 miles).

From Graffham ride W, N and NW to the lane crossroads at grid ref. 910190. Then ride via Heyshott (grid ref. 898181) onto the unmetalled lane at the foot of the Downs which runs W to the main road at Cocking on the A286 (grid ref. 878175). Cross the main

road and take lanes at the foot of the Downs, just N of due W, via
Bepton, Didling and Treyford to Elsted (grid ref. 816196). Retrace
your way as far back E as Bepton, where you strike NNE along the
lane to **Midhurst** (31 miles).

From Midhurst take the lane that runs just S of the bank of the
Rother via South Ambersham to Selham (grid ref. 935207). Ride S
and then SW on lanes to meet the A285 at grid ref. 965185. Turn
left, then almost immediately right on lanes again via Burton Mill
Pond to the lane crossroads at grid ref. 982178. Here turn right,
riding S via Sutton End and Sutton and then SW to Bignor (grid
ref. 983143). Ride SE via West Burton and Bury, where you cross
the A29, and then SSE to join the B2139 at Houghton (grid ref.
018115), turning left for **Amberley station** (46 miles).

Trains run from Amberley to London Victoria or via Ford to
Brighton and Portsmouth.

Out of Barnham – one more railway station on the flat,
glasshouse-glittering, horticultural, beach-hut-bearing,
crowded coastal strip – out of Barnham, and through
Walberton with its heterogeneous housing (the mixture of
dates and styles and fabrics put me in mind of Kent), and
up to Slindon. Slindon has its architectural variety and
vagaries, too, including a thatched railway carriage which
does duty as a summerhouse, but it is essentially a flint
village of the Downs. It marks a boundary. It is a sloping
village, set into the hill, and you have to climb up into it,
out of the plain.

Beyond, you go on climbing, with woods one side of the
road and open farmland the other. Then you drop a little,
into Eartham, before rising gently once more into the
extensive plantation of Eartham Wood towards the top of
the ridge.

Here, we leave metalled lanes for a while, following
Roman Stane Street, clearly marked at its outset with a
noticeboard giving historical and technical details about

the road. It ran inland from the port of Chichester (Noviomagus) to London. Fishbourne, near Chichester, has a famous Roman palace, and another villa (less celebrated, but with interesting mosaic work and lying in a quite unspoiled landscape) is at Bignor: this is linked to Stane Street by a steeply dropping spur road. The bridleway – well laid, passable on a bike in all but the wettest conditions – follows the Roman route due north-east for a little over two miles. Today, it was too brilliantly, cheerfully sunny for us to summon up that grim mood in which one imagines the Roman legionaries, miserable mercenary expatriates, trudging through alien Britain. Indeed, in May sunshine and warmth the West Sussex Downs are as good a place to be, surely, as anywhere even in Tuscany or Umbria – and I imagine that in summer the Romans of Bignor must often have felt as content as exiles ever can.

When the track leaves the road in Eartham Woods, it runs at first through beech trees. Patches of May light dappled the path carpeted with honey-coloured catkins. Then you emerge into open country, though at first trees and bushes continue to fringe the path. Kate and I stopped to make tea, here where the prospects begin to broaden and the full delight of this lovely walk begins to be felt. The corn was green: but we recalled how some years earlier, camping with our children at Coldharbour, we had walked here in August and seen a pair of deer break from their cover in tall ripe yellow wheat and crash across the field to the woods on the ridge above.

Just west of Bignor Hill, at the summit of your walk, a number of paths and tracks intersect. A wooden signpost gives the mileage to some of the old Roman destinations. Cars can park here, having laboured up the steep tree-shadowed lane from Bignor village, and the immediate surroundings may be quite crowded. However, once you wander a mile or so west you are likely to find yourselves alone to enjoy the turf, thorn-bushes, white chalk tracks and views over to the Weald. Below, steep hangers – untended woods thick with creepers and fallen trees – grow all down the scarp. We stayed up on the tops for the night:

South Downs above Sutton, 7.00pm, 26 May 1990

We're sitting by a chalk track that glows brilliant white in the evening sun. The springy turf has orchids, cowslips, buttercups, moss – and too many other flowers whose names I don't know. I'm equally ignorant about the birds I hear singing in the hanger. Except for the throaty cooing of the wood pigeon, which comes again and again from far down the hillside, I don't recognise their songs.

Kate is sitting ten yards away, facing into the sun, drawing: Jude and Maddy have given her pastels and charcoals for her birthday, which is today.

In the hour and a half we have been here, no one has passed. Yet we're not more than two miles from the NT car park. (Research proves that most people won't willingly venture more than, is it 300 yards, from their cars.) Well: there can be few walks in England as beautiful as the walk we have taken since leaving the lane in Eartham Wood. And I've never been up here on so clear a day: looking back as we passed Gumber Farm – flinty, somnolent, with its fine barns – we saw the Isle of Wight beyond the Solent.

Here, we are at the scrubby, attractive edge of a wood, and below begins the wood proper: yew, rowan, ash, hazel. Bordering the path, the tussocky turf is overgrown with brambles, and with may – may, often tinged with pink, heavily scented, is everywhere. Usual half-sadness of May and June: so much vernal life: it feels excessive, transient. When June runs into July, dusty and tawny, summer's almost gone.

I love this wooded landscape, where fields run to the edge of thick woods. Corn still dark green. Here and there a lighter note, a paler stretch of hay (?silage grass).

Standing up, strolling, I can see the Downs running away west, and to the north – beyond the flat country where we will cycle tomorrow – rises the sandy Weald (earlier we saw the vivid brass-yellow glint of a sand quarry). Is that highest Wealden hill Blackdown (280m), one of the highest points in the south of England? From up here all of it, hills and plain, looks slumbrous, lyrically wooded.

Later, as dusk fell, a nightingale sang to us from the thickets.

Less melodious was a savage cry that broke the silence of the small hours. A thundering rumble down the track above us, the thud of wheels landing (after a mid-air flight) back on the packed chalk, this wild half-joyful howl, more thunder of wheels down the steep hill below: we sat up in our sleeping bags. What could it be?

'A mountain biker,' I assured Kate.

'At this time? There isn't even a moon. Do they ride with lights?' (We ascertained later that some of them do.)

'It must have been a mountain biker. What else could it have been?' I reasoned.

'Do you think he was *enjoying* himself?'

'I should think he was rather surprised by that rut.'

'By the time he arrived there after that downhill run, he must have been doing twenty miles an hour at least. If you did that on an ordinary touring bike you'd end up with a wheelful of smashed spokes, for sure.'

Such was our pillow talk as we drifted back into sleep. Then at seven next morning, as we sat drinking tea, we were privileged to see as well as hear not just one but nine airborne traumas as nine mountain bikers, rolling down the long slope, flashing through the open gate, hit the leading edge of the deep rut beside us, took off, and – ouf! – landed. The last of the group found enough presence of mind, after the inevitable grunt/howl, to half-turn in the saddle and call out: 'Is this the South Downs Way?' But he was speeding out of earshot, into the fourth dimension of his next confrontation with the geosphere, by the time we shouted out that No, it wasn't.

Even the most determined seeker after adversity could find nothing strenuous in the day's ride that lay before us now – nothing strenuous, that is, apart from the sharp drop down the chalk-and-clay hollow-way from the signpost to Coldharbour Farm. We dug our heels in to hold back our gravity-tugged, laden bikes. Then you are out of the woods, at Coldharbour, and looking down that hidden valley; then dropping through it, and over the stream bridge, and swinging west along the foot of the scarp. That is the theme of much of this day's route: lanes snaking along the scarp foot, sometimes hedged and shady, sometimes open, sometimes right up against the rising ground and sometimes separated from where the slope begins by a field of grain or sheep or horses, but again and again shadowing, in their twists and curves, the shifting line of the Downs. Then, especially heading back east, there are contrasting stretches, further from the hills, where you cross sandy heathland, with birches and oaks, and rhododendrons in fiery purple bloom running back like flames into the woodland. The chalk track from Heyshott to the main road at Cocking is rough going, but everywhere else the lanes were smooth, humming, crunchy with dry gravel, their black tar getting sticky in the strengthening sun.

The three downland churches – Didling, Elsted, Selham – add interest to the ride. Elsted has herring-bone masonry, a Saxon technique unfortunately not reproduced in the restoration work done on this much-damaged, much-restored church. Nearby is an attractive stable, with a lantern, converted into a residence, a good example of the brick-and-clunch fabric you may already have observed, for instance at pretty Haslands Farm near Barlavington. ('Clunch' is the layer of hard chalk often used, in Sussex and elsewhere, as a building material.)

Selham church has herring-bone masonry, too. Inside, there is an unusual, pre-Raphaelite-inspired memorial plaque to the son of the Lacaita family, local landowners: a Spanish name, a Jewish name? This boy, killed in Flanders in 1918, would seem to have been the last of the line.

Didling is the most memorable of the churches. Dedicated to Saint Andrew, it is a single-celled building dating mostly from the thirteenth century (though a Saxon font survives). It is attractively plain: as the notes you can buy there rightly state, 'the simple, bright and whitewashed interior, with its tiled floors and plaster ceilings, feel homely, lived-in and unspoilt.' It has a fine setting, just towards the hills from the lane. Both times I have been there, sheep grazing in the field behind have given point to the name, 'the Shepherds' Church', by which it is known. When I was there with Kate, a group of Girl Guides were encamped in another neighbouring field. One of their fretted leaders voiced the usual adult complaint: 'They're not walking at all, you know. You get them up to the top, and they just sit there. They're hardly walking at all.' Indolence, in the late May sun, was very understandable. We lengthened out our early lunch break with coffee and a doze on the churchyard bench.

After Midhurst, riding back east, you are near the bank of the Rother. This is sandy country, as sandy almost as east Suffolk, and like the Suffolk Sandlings (see Route 3) it needs watering in summer. Sand gathers in the lanes and whirls in the breeze and seems generally to be escaping from the fields. A tributary stream above South Ambersham has been harnessed for irrigation, and there are pipes and revolving sprays in the laneside fields.

Polo is played here. Horses lord it over some of the best West Sussex pastures. Near the start of this day's ride, after the lovely streamside lane past Duncton, after Seaford College with its prefabs and cricket pavilions, you come to a perfect parkland by East Lavington: a stud farm, in Arcady. At Ambersham, of course, the Duke himself plays, with the international polo set from England, West Germany, Argentina. There was a match on the afternoon we rode past. I once saw a chukka or two, made intelligible to the lay understanding by a simultaneous loudspeaker commentary in a suitably plummy voice. It seemed a lively game, jolly hard on the horses. Its skills are probably tricky to master. In the morning, near Graffham, Kate and I chanced to see an aspirant at practice. The man galloped purposefully up, swung his stick, and missed the ball altogether. Perhaps he didn't have blue blood.

More heaths and woods, and some attractive estate cottages, lie beyond Selham with its lost little pub, The Three Moles, a suitably withdrawing yet convivial name. Then across the main road to Burton Mill Pond. I assume that the mill once drove an iron-working hammer. Now it has reopened and grinds organic flour, which you can buy there. Usually this is a quiet place (though on this Bank Holiday Monday there were a dozen or so cars parked), where you can sit on the edge of the pond with your back against the wooden fence, drink tea, and watch the waterbirds, the pale water patched with lily-leaves running back among reedbeds into wooded banks, the line of the Downs above, and the sky.

From here, you might take the last seven or eight miles to Amberley station in one easy go. Or you might make the most of the daylight and stay as late as possible in this lovely stretch of country. (Alternatively – though it closes in late afternoon, of course – you may find you have time to visit Bignor Roman villa.)

There are plenty of strolls in the heaths and woods by Sutton, and ramblers are invited to wander over Coates Common (just east of the crossroads above Burton Mill Pond). One pleasant walk is along the paths and bridleways and tracks of Bignor Park, not a grand country house, but a place that has eluded change. Nothing much seems to have altered there since, as a child, I rode my twenty-inch two-wheeler along its flinty drive.

Route 12:

West Sussex Downs and Lower Greensand Hills

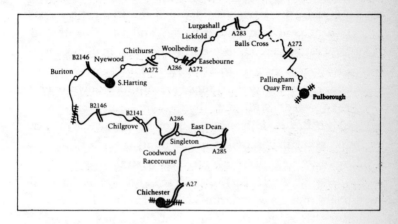

Chichester to Pulborough

The first part of this route parallels the first part of Route 11. You are up in the West Sussex Downs. This time, you are following metalled lanes rather than tracks (apart from a stretch of unmade byway just before you drop to Buriton at the foot of the scarp). And these lanes are some of the quietest, yet most scenic, in southern England.

Climbing up to Goodwood from Chichester, the road is wide and may be quite busy with holiday traffic. (It will certainly be busy should you make the mistake of choosing this route when there is a race meeting on.) East from the racecourse, life gets quieter. Then once you turn back west again, by oddly-named Droke, first of several flinty downland hamlets, you are following an empty single-track road. There are brief busier stretches at West Dean and Chilgrove, but essentially what lies before you now is fifteen miles of peaceful and mostly level cycling through the heart of the wooded, corn-growing top of West Sussex.

Once off the Downs, we ride fairly directly across the scarp foot country (explored at leisure in Route 11) to reach the hills of the Lower Greensand. Less broken and dramatic than the High Weald which marks East Sussex's border with Kent (see Routes 6, 7, 9 and 10), this upland of north-west Sussex none the less includes, in Blackdown Hill (280 metres), the highest point in south-east England. Jude and I had energetic riding here: up and down over sandhills towards Midhurst, then a long haul, climbing 500 feet, to Bexley Hill, just south of Blackdown. However, the impression that remains in my mind is less of hills than of sandy heathy woods and sandy sunken lanes. Seen from on top of the Downs, the Weald and Greensand Hills hereabouts make a wonderfully wooded scene. Down among the trees, you ride along canopied lanes dappled with light and shade. Towards Pulborough, in flatter and lower-lying country on the west bank of the Arun, making for the bridge (open to walkers and riders only) which takes you across the river, you are at the edge of the Mens wood. Peter Brandon (*The Sussex Landscape*) cites the Mens as one of those 'anciently enclosed woods or commons' which 'still convey a sense of the "dark and impenetrable wild" that early writers envisaged' when they wrote of the old Wealden forests.

This is two days' steady riding: seventy-one miles, with some long and some steep climbs. We stayed overnight at my brother and sister-in-law's house near Compton. Compton, Buriton and South Harting all have bed and breakfast places (where you should book well ahead in summer, as the South Downs Way runs by here).

Two days should allow most riders to complete this route, for it can easily be shortened. The final section can be made quicker and more straightforward if you stay on metalled lanes after Ebernoe and Balls Cross (details are in the itinerary, below) and pick up your train at Billingshurst, rather than taking tracks and going further south to Pulborough (but if you do opt for Billingshurst, you will have about two and a half miles on the A272, a main road though not a fearfully busy one).

Drawing out the route on the OS map, you will see that the first part (after Goodwood) consists of a large loop out east and then back west, easily shortened or virtually omitted. Another loop, along an unmade road and down via Buriton, takes you from Compton to South Harting: doing this directly by the B road would save you eight or nine miles and the best part of an hour's ride.

So you have various ways of shortening your journey. Alternatively, you might linger a little, perhaps visiting the outdoor Weald and Downland Museum at Singleton (you pass the entrance as you ride into West Dean), or perhaps detouring after Lurgashall to visit Petworth House and Park: the park was landscaped by Capability Brown and pictures in the house include some by Turner. Choosing to make two overnight stops would give you a more expansive and flexible schedule. This is certainly a ride, and a part of England, well worth taking your time over.

Chichester to Pulborough

Distance: approx. 71 miles. OS 197

Duration: Two days (one or two overnight stops)

Terrain: Some easy stretches, but also some long and some steep climbs, so the route as a whole is strenuous. Use is made of bridleways and unmade roads. In the first case, between Compton and South Harting, an alternative and more direct route on the B2146 is evident on the map. In the second case, after Balls Cross, an alternative route on metalled lanes is given (to Billingshurst rather than Pulborough). After rain, and in the winter, the alternatives on metalled roads should be taken in any event, as the tracks will be muddy.

Itinerary: Trains run to **Chichester** from London Victoria and also from Brighton and Portsmouth.

From Chichester station, walk up towards the town centre, turning right at the Market Cross. Ride out NE, following signs for the A27 Brighton road. On the outskirts of the town you will come to a roundabout (grid ref. 877059) with a lane off left signposted to Goodwood. Follow this lane, taking left at T-junction, and climb steadily past the motor racetrack/aerodrome to Goodwood Racecourse (grid ref. 885110). The lane divides as you approach the course: take the right-hand fork, follow the S side of the course, and continue E via Pilleygreen Lodges (grid ref. 904116) and the picnic site at Selhurst Park to reach the main A285 Petworth road at grid ref. 939120 (10 miles).

Take the main road N for less than 1 mile, turning off left before Upwaltham cottages and following this single-track lane W via Droke (grid ref. 924128), East Dean and Charlton to the main road at Singleton (grid ref. 877132). Follow the main road W and curving S through West Dean. Turn off right at grid ref. 857125, on a lane signposted to Colworth Down. Climb through twists and curves in an overall NW direction to Colworth Down (grid ref. 846146), then via Stapleash Farm to left turn at grid ref. 836155, and so down to Chilgrove on the B2141. Follow the B road NW, climbing steadily up Chilgrove Hill to turn off left at grid ref. 818148 to **East Marden** (26 miles).

Ride NW and N on lane from East Marden to Newbuildings crossroads, taking left here and riding just N of due W to reach the B2146 at grid ref. 771156, just N of Compton. Turn right along the B road, then almost immediately left, at grid ref. 770158. This lane soon forks: take the right fork, which is signposted 'Unsuitable for Motor Vehicles'. Metalled as far as Cowdown Farm, this then becomes a 'Soft Public road': follow it almost due W to the crossroads at grid ref. 739155. Here cross the railway line and immediately turn right on the lane which, following the railway at first, runs N through woods to Buriton (grid ref. 737203). From Buriton ride NE to reach the B2146 at grid ref. 757217, turning right and riding via Nursted to **South Harting** (41 miles).

Leave South Harting on the lane which runs NNE to Nyewood (grid ref. 803218). Just beyond Nyewood take the single-track lane right via Dumpford to reach the A272 by Trotton Common (grid ref. 838223). Turn right for 100 yards or so on this main road, then left on the lane across the Rother to Chithurst. Follow this lane as it swings E and runs more or less parallel to the A272 through Woolbeding (grid ref. 873228) and across the A286 to **Easebourne** (grid ref. 895225) (50 miles).

Take the lane that climbs steadily out of Easebourne to the NE, via Bexleyhill (grid ref. 913253), and so dropping again to Lickfold (grid ref. 926262). Ride via Lurgashall (grid ref. 937272) to the A283 Petworth to Northchapel road, at grid ref. 953280. Turn right and after about 1 mile turn left on lanes again, to Ebernoe (grid ref. 975280). At the next lane junction, turn right, and ride just E of S to **Balls Cross** (grid ref. 987263) (61 miles).

From here there is an *alternative route to Billingshurst* as follows: take lanes via Kirdford (grid ref. 016266) to Wisborough Green (grid ref. 050260), then E on the A272 to Billingshurst, for trains to London Victoria or via Ford to Brighton and Portsmouth (total distance via this alternative route: 70 miles).

The *main route* is as follows: from Balls Cross take lane towards Kirdford, but almost at once fork off right on the bridle path (initially well surfaced but soft later) which runs via Crawfold Farm ESE to join lanes at grid ref. 014253. Ride SE and then S, taking left fork where the lane divides, and reaching the A272 at grid ref. 023238. Cross over the main road and ride on lane through the wood to T-junction at grid ref. 035235. Turn right and follow lane in generally southerly and SW direction until (at grid ref. 027220) you reach the waymarked bridleway off left to Pallingham Quay Farm (grid ref. 036216). Cross the river and the abandoned canal, and then, via a dogleg on bridle path and track S and then E, reach the lane at grid ref. 042210. Follow this lane S and then E: it swings under the railway line, and just past the rail bridge a waymarked footpath leads off right. Wheel your bike along this footpath until

you come out by the forecourt of **Pulborough station** (71 miles).
Trains run to London Victoria and to Brighton and Portsmouth.

In a move which too few English towns seem likely to
emulate, Chichester not long ago banned cars from its
central area. The great charm of this little cathedral city
(no more than a town in size and numbers) is once again
immediately evident – more evident than it was when I
used to visit it as a child, for thirty-odd years ago motor
traffic was already suffocating it. Now everyone, tourist or
native, can see and enjoy how the medievalism of the
ecclesiastical quarter, echoed in the early sixteenth-century
Market Cross, blends with the eighteenth-century solidity
of the town centre's public and residential buildings.

A stroll through the wide streets as you buy food for
your picnic, a cup of coffee before setting off: this is how a
cycle trip ought to begin. But in most towns of this size,
including my home town of Lewes, the county town of
East Sussex as Chichester is of West, you are best advised
to get out quickly onto the lanes, rather than lingering
amidst noise and exhaust fumes.

Recent town planning in Chichester seems to have been
along continental lines. There is a peripheral zone of
commerce and light industry – inevitably a rather
anonymous region of instant buildings. One roundabout
presents a characteristic set of options: 'Superstore,
Industrial Estate, Crematorium'. However, zoning of this
kind is obviously the key to keeping town centres quiet and
traffic-free.

It is steady work up to Goodwood. Jude's perseverance (he
stayed on the bike in low gears rather than getting off to
push) augured well, and indeed he was hardly to get off or

complain throughout the seventy miles. Not big for his age, but mega-tough.

The road climbs past commercialised leisure sites: motor racetrack and aerodrome, golf course, and then the horse-racing circuit at the summit. When there is no race meeting, the track is opened as a campsite. It would make a fine base for Downland cycle-touring (you could put together parts of this route and of Route 11 to give three or four days' riding on the tops and along the scarp foot).

As you ride east, there are views over the coastal plain towards the sea, intermittent at first as fire-breaks or gaps in planting interrupt the mixed woods, then continuous when open country replaces forests to the south of the lane. On the other side, wooden picnic tables and grassy glades are set among the trees. You could sit here and watch the changing light on the Channel as you ate and relaxed. We were there on a Thursday in the third week of August, and while there were a good few people about, neither the road nor the woods felt crowded.

Quieter riding comes as you swing back west through Droke and East Dean. Even in high summer, with occasional tourists nosing along the lanes by car, this string of settlements has a remote feel. Flint catches grey light and can make the sunshine look cold, bringing out an underlying austerity in these villages. This would be a desolate landscape in winter: damp November winds scurrying along the hollow plateau from the west, trees shedding their last leaves, the grey sky lowering between the ridges to north and south, and the clay-with-flints of the soil gleaming through thin corn.

For the moment, we were sitting in golden stubble. Between the dark green of the woods clothing the slopes, the fields of the dry valley were golden. The land was

parched. Seeing sheep on a background of tawny, almost
purple hillside, I had to look twice before believing that
they were in a piece of pasture rather than on bare earth.
July had been the driest (so I read the next morning in the
Stores at South Harting) for forty years. Rain would be
welcome. And rain was coming. You could see it in the
clouds piled against the pale blue: mercury, lead, silver – a
vivid contrast to the green-and-gold landscape. And you
could smell it in the wind, freshening, cool enough for us
to have chosen the shelter of a hedge-bank and a giant
straw-bale when we were looking for a place for lunch.

Rain, and hail too, caught up with us at Singleton.
Down past a flint terrace, with wallflowers in beds by the
lane and runner beans and giant onions in a vegetable
patch by the church gate, you come to the Saxon church
of St Mary. What caught our eye was the marble
memorial to local huntsman Tom Johnson, which is on the
wall opposite the door. Its text is strangely compounded of
aristocratic condescension, moral sententiousness and love
of hunting:

> Here IOHNSON lies what Hunter can deny
> Old, honest TOM the Tribute of a Sigh.
> Deaf is that Ear, which caught the op'ning sound
> Dumb is that Tongue, which cheard the Hills around.
> Unpleasing Truth Death hunts us from our Birth
> In view, and Men, like Foxes, take to Earth.

'Old, honest TOM' died in 1744 and this monument,
which records that his virtues 'recommended him to the
service and gain'd him the approbation of several of the
nobility', was set up by his last employer.

Hailstones were melting on the warm path and rain was
steaming on the warm road when we came out of the
church. Riding on, along lanes which dipped and rose and
zig-zagged across more broken country, we were sheltered

from another heavy shower by the belt of thick trees
overhanging us as we climbed above West Dean. Little
enough water, though, after so long a drought. But it left
the evening sky fresh and clear, with sharp-edged clouds
sailing in the breeze and the air cooler than it had been for
weeks.

The next morning, bright but still cool, began with a stroll
along a green lane. Like the Suffolk bridleway described in
Route 4, this track (far less overgrown) ran between
parallel rows of mature trees, suggesting some time-worn
field boundary or drove road. Back on metalled lanes, we
enjoyed an easy run to Buriton, through small fields where
the downland scrub was encroaching on the sheep-grazing,
and under the boughs of fine beechwoods. There were no
signs of the storm damage suffered by so many of Sussex's
more exposed or more neglected plantations. This was a
thriving wood, with well-spaced trees just maturing. I
think the grandest beeches I know grow on the gravels of
the lower Seine valley, but beeches have a great affinity for
chalk, too, and in chalk downland they are the dominant
broadleaf species. Here where they bordered the lane the
light beneath them was so delicately green, the ground so
enticingly patterned with sun and shade, that Jude and I
could not resist stopping for a cup of coffee (even though
we had had breakfast only forty minutes earlier). Sitting
chatting on the bank of the lane was a way of making the
woods last longer.

The trees begin to change, with the soil, as soon as you
drop off the scarp. By the time we had crossed the
flatlands of the Rother valley, and were climbing to
Chithurst, we were in a new landscape, with hazel and ash
and holly and above all oak growing in the loose sand, and
the high lane-banks covered often with bracken.

Chithurst is due north of Didling, and only three or four
miles away. Each village has a small, old church. Near
neighbours though they are, St Andrew's at Didling
(which we visited in Route 11) and St Mary's at Chithurst
have entirely different settings. The few churchyard trees
at St Andrew's, though they include a fine yew, cannot
dispel the sense that the building stands open to the sky.
It lies above a bare lane, on the dry chalk just at the
spring-line. Above, sheep graze and beeches grow on the
abrupt, uncomplicated scarp. At Chithurst, you are deep
in mixed woods, and the churchyard overlooks the green,
swift Rother. Climbing away to the north, you would rise
and fall among tangled, sandy hills.

We turned not north but east, stopping beside a
tributary of the Rother, one of the hammer streams that
drove the old Wealden iron workings. There is a Buddhist
monastery in a country house at Chithurst and the land
beside the stream appeared to belong to this, too. There
was open access to glades by the water, downstream of the
bridge. We sat on the grass and ate, and just as we
finished our meal a tiny shrew, much smaller than my
thumb, came hopping among the grassblades to tidy up
our crumbs. It seemed quite unafraid of humans (through
ignorance of their ways, I suppose) and went on to sniff
around among our bicycle wheels and water bottles.

Upstream of the bridge is the hammer pond. The sluices
are no longer in place. Green water foamed to white as it
tumbled over the weir. Here was an echo that brought out
the underlying unity of the varied Sussex landscape, for I
was at once reminded of the pond I had sat beside last
autumn in Sheffield Forest (see Route 8). I refer to that as
a 'mill pond', but it is at least as likely to have driven an
iron-hammer as a corn-mill. The two ponds' settings
amidst silent mixed woods mirror each other across the

intervening thirty-five miles, and across the modern division of Sussex into West and East.

Riding towards Easebourne, above Midhurst, we had views across fields and copses to the Downs. Three deer, startled by our bicycles, sprang from above the lane-bank and crashed (startling us) across a brown field of dried flax plants. Sand, washed out of the banks by the previous day's rainstorms, lay in ripples across the lane. Jude pointed out to me where old walls of sandstone blocks underlaid and supported the banks. These walls are no longer being kept up and the sand is slipping into the roads.

After Easebourne, no quiet lanes run due east, and you can no longer run parallel to the Rother (and the main Petworth road). We zig-zagged up past handsome estate cottages with distinctive bright gold-painted windowframes. Reaching the top of Bexley Hill, below Blackdown, you get no panorama as a reward. All the height you have worked to gain is squandered in a headlong descent into Lickfold – you have to brake hard to hold the bike back. But the climb, through heath and woods and bracken, is a pleasure in itself.

Then come quiet, spacious villages, as the land grows flatter towards the Arun gap: Lurgashall, where we had ginger beer outside the Noah's Ark, and Ebernoe, lost in woods, its cricket pitch on the green bisected (so it seemed) by the lane we rode down. I wondered whether, on match days, veteran club members in white flannels sit on green metal chairs in the carriageway and make passing cars wait till the over ends before allowing them through?

By an unmade track through farmland and forestry plantation and woods, and on lanes across the Petworth road and through the fringe of the deep Mens wood, we came to the peaceful river-crossing which made a last highlight on this constantly attractive route. Pallingham Quay Farm is signposted left down a bridle path. You find it standing on the edge of water-meadows. As the name suggests, there was waterborne trade on the Arun once. A canal which runs alongside it and sometimes merges with it used to link it with the Wey. Now both the canal and the stream which joins the river here were dry: while the stream no doubt flows in winter, the canal was reed-choked and derelict.

As you cross the old stone bridges that span all three watercourses, the Downs, which have been hidden by woods these last several miles of low-lying riding, come into view again. What you see now is not the range that runs west into Hampshire, but the eastward stretch towards Chanctonbury and Ditchling Beacon and Lewes.

The line of hills seemed to be calling me home. The grey-green meadow, rustling in the breeze, open but melancholy under the greying sky, felt like the right place to say a silent goodbye – goodbye not just to West Sussex, for some weeks or months, but to all the rides for this book, which had given me so much. Even here, in a part of England I thought I knew well, the search for back ways and unfrequented tracks had led me once again to a new and memorable scene. I was at the centre of a triangle formed by three main roads: A272, A29, A283 – they stand out on the OS map as if they would dominate their surroundings. But I could hear no sounds but natural sounds, and what I could see was probably not much changed from what a bargee or wayfarer a century and a half ago would have seen.

Appendix

Useful Addresses

The Cyclists' Touring Club
Cotterell House
69 Meadrow
Godalming
Surrey GU7 3HS

East Anglia Tourist Board
Toppesfield Hall
Hadleigh
Suffolk IP7 5DN

South East England Tourist Board
The Old Brew House
Warwick Park
Tunbridge Wells
Kent TN2 5TU

Stanford's (Maps)
14 Long Acre
London WC2P 9LP

Youth Hostels Association of England and Wales
Trevelyan House
8 St Stephen's Hill
St Albans
Hertfordshire

Booklist

First I give some titles on cycling, cycle maintenance and cycle touring which may prove useful. Then comes a list of the works I consulted in the writing of this book: many of these are now out of print but I would like to record my indebtedness to their authors.

Richard Ballantine, *Richard's Bicycle Book* (Pan)

Peter Dobson, *The Corgi Book of Bicycles and Bicycling* (Corgi)

Christa Gausden and Nicholas Crane, *The CTC Route Guide to Cycling in Britain and Ireland* (Penguin)

Martin Ryle, *By Bicycle in Ireland* (Impact Books)

Roderick Watson and Martin Gray, *The Penguin Book of the Bicycle* (Penguin)

Patrick Armstrong, *The Changing Landscape: The History and Ecology of Man's Impact on the Face of East Anglia* (Terence Dalton, Lavenham, Suffolk, 1975)

Peter Brandon, *The Sussex Landscape* (Hodder, London, 1974)

Paul Burnham and Stuart McRae, *Kent: The Garden of England* (Norbury, Tenterden, Kent, 1978)

William Cobbett, *Rural Rides* (Everyman edition)

W G Hoskins, *The Making of the English Landscape* (Hodder, London, 1969)

Edward A Martin, *Sussex Geology* (Archer, London, 1932)

Richard Church, *Kent* (Robert Hale, London, 1946)

H J Massingham, *English Downland* (Batsford, London, 1936)

S G McRae and C P Burnham, *The Rural Landscape of Kent* (Wye College, Wye, Kent, 1973)

N Pevsner, *Suffolk* (in the 'Buildings of England' series) (Penguin, 1975)

Norman Scarfe, *Suffolk* (Hodder, London, 1972)

H D Westacott, *The South Downs Way* (Penguin, Harmondsworth, 1983)

John Talbot White, *The South-East Down and Weald: Kent, Surrey and Sussex* (Eyre Methuen, London, 1977)

Index